ESSAYS OF TRAVEL

ESSAYS OF TRAVEL

ROBERT LOUIS STEVENSON

MANOR

ROCKVILLE, MARYLAND

2009

ISBN: 978-1-60450-359-3

Published by Arc Manor
P. O. Box 10339
Rockville, MD 20849-0339
www.ArcManor.com

Printed in the United States of America/United Kingdom

Contents

CHAPTER I—THE AMATEUR EMIGRANT

The Second Cabin

I first encountered my fellow-passengers on the Broomielaw in Glasgow. Thence we descended the Clyde in no familiar spirit, but looking askance on each other as on possible enemies. A few Scandinavians, who had already grown acquainted on the North Sea, were friendly and voluble over their long pipes; but among English speakers distance and suspicion reigned supreme. The sun was soon overclouded, the wind freshened and grew sharp as we continued to descend the widening estuary; and with the falling temperature the gloom among the passengers increased. Two of the women wept. Any one who had come aboard might have supposed we were all absconding from the law. There was scarce a word interchanged, and no common sentiment but that of cold united us, until at length, having touched at Greenock, a pointing arm and a rush to the starboard now announced that our ocean steamer was in sight. There she lay in mid-river, at the Tail of the Bank, her sea-signal flying: a wall of bulwark, a street of white deck-houses, an aspiring forest of spars, larger than a church, and soon to be as populous as many an incorporated town in the land to which she was to bear us.

I was not, in truth, a steerage passenger. Although anxious to see the worst of emigrant life, I had some work to finish on the voyage, and was advised to go by the second cabin, where at least I should have a table at command. The advice was excellent; but to understand the choice, and what I gained, some outline of the internal disposition of the ship will first be necessary. In her very nose is Steerage No. 1, down two pair of stairs. A little abaft, another companion, labelled Steerage No. 2 and 3, gives admission to three galleries, two running forward towards Steerage No. 1, and the third aft towards the engines. The starboard forward gallery is the second cabin. Away abaft the engines and below the officers' cabins, to complete our survey of the vessel, there is yet a third nest of steerages, labelled 4 and 5. The second cabin, to return, is thus a modified oasis in the very heart of the steerages. Through the thin partition you can hear the steerage passengers being sick, the rattle of tin dishes as they sit at meals, the varied accents in which they converse, the crying of their children terrified by this new experience, or the clean flat smack of the parental hand in chastisement.

There are, however, many advantages for the inhabitant of this strip. He does not require to bring his own bedding or dishes, but finds berths and a table completely if somewhat roughly furnished. He enjoys a distinct superiority in diet; but this, strange to say, differs not only on different ships, but on the same ship according as her head is to the east or west. In my own experience, the principal difference between our table and that of the true steerage passenger was the table itself, and the crockery plates from which we ate. But lest I should show myself ungrateful, let me recapitulate every advantage. At breakfast we had a choice between tea and coffee for beverage; a choice not easy to make, the two were so surprisingly alike. I found that I could sleep after the coffee and lay awake after the tea, which is proof conclusive of some chemical disparity; and even by the palate I could distinguish a smack of snuff in the former from a flavour of boiling and dish-cloths in the second. As a matter of fact, I have seen passengers, after many sips, still doubting which had been supplied them. In the way of eatables at the same meal we were gloriously favoured; for in addition to porridge, which was common to all, we had Irish stew, sometimes a bit of fish, and sometimes rissoles. The dinner of soup, roast fresh beef, boiled salt junk, and potatoes, was, I believe, exactly common to the steerage and the second cabin; only I have heard it rumoured that our potatoes were of a superior brand; and twice a week, on pudding-days, instead of duff, we had a saddle-bag filled with currants under the name of a plum-pudding. At tea we were served with some broken meat from the saloon; sometimes in the comparatively elegant form of spare patties or rissoles; but as a general thing mere chicken-bones and flakes of fish, neither hot nor cold. If these were not the scrapings of plates their looks belied them sorely; yet we were all too hungry to be proud, and fell to these leavings greedily. These, the bread, which was excellent, and the soup and porridge which were both good, formed my whole diet throughout the voyage; so that except for the broken meat and the convenience of a table I might as well have been in the steerage outright. Had they given me porridge again in the evening, I should have been perfectly contented with the fare. As it was, with a few biscuits and some whisky and water before turning in, I kept my body going and my spirits up to the mark.

The last particular in which the second cabin passenger remarkably stands ahead of his brother of the steerage is one altogether of sentiment. In the steerage there are males and females; in the second cabin ladies and gentlemen. For some time after I came aboard I thought I was only a male; but in the course of a voyage of discovery between decks, I came on a brass plate, and learned that I was still a gentleman. Nobody knew it, of course. I was lost in the crowd of males and females, and rigorously confined to the same quarter of the deck. Who could tell whether I housed on the port or starboard side of steerage No. 2 and 3? And it was only there that my superiority became practical; everywhere else I was incognito, moving among my inferiors with simplicity, not so much as a swagger to indicate that I was a gentleman after all, and had broken meat to tea. Still, I was like one with a patent of nobility in a drawer at home; and when I felt out of spirits I could go down and refresh myself with a look of that brass plate.

For all these advantages I paid but two guineas. Six guineas is the steerage fare; eight that by the second cabin; and when you remember that the steerage passenger must supply bedding and dishes, and, in five cases out of ten, either brings some dainties with him, or privately pays the steward for extra rations, the difference in price becomes almost nominal. Air comparatively fit to breathe, food comparatively varied, and the satisfaction of being still privately a gentleman, may thus be had almost for the asking. Two of my fellow-passengers in the second cabin had already made the passage by the cheaper fare, and declared it was an experiment not to be repeated. As I go on to tell about my steerage friends, the reader will perceive that they were not alone in their opinion. Out of ten with whom I was more or less intimate, I am sure not fewer than five vowed, if they returned, to travel second cabin; and all who had left their wives behind them assured me they would go without the comfort of their presence until they could afford to bring them by saloon.

Our party in the second cabin was not perhaps the most interesting on board. Perhaps even in the saloon there was as much good-will and character. Yet it had some elements of curiosity. There was a mixed group of Swedes, Danes, and Norsemen, one of whom, generally known by the name of 'Johnny,' in spite of his own protests, greatly diverted us by his clever, cross-country efforts to speak English, and became on the strength of that an universal favourite—it takes so little in this world of shipboard to create a popularity. There was, besides, a Scots mason, known from his favourite dish as 'Irish Stew,' three or four nondescript Scots, a fine young Irishman, O'Reilly, and a pair of young men who deserve a special word of condemnation. One of them was Scots; the other claimed to be American; admitted, after some fencing, that he was born in England; and ultimately proved to be an Irishman born and nurtured, but ashamed to own his country. He had a sister on board, whom he faithfully neglected throughout the voyage, though she was not only sick, but much his senior, and had nursed and cared for him in childhood. In appearance he was like an imbecile Henry the Third of France. The Scotsman, though perhaps as big an ass, was not so dead of heart; and I have only bracketed them together because they were fast friends, and disgraced themselves equally by their conduct at the table.

Next, to turn to topics more agreeable, we had a newly-married couple, devoted to each other, with a pleasant story of how they had first seen each other years ago at a preparatory school, and that very afternoon he had carried her books home for her. I do not know if this story will be plain to southern readers; but to me it recalls many a school idyll, with wrathful swains of eight and nine confronting each other stride-legs, flushed with jealousy; for to carry home a young lady's books was both a delicate attention and a privilege.

Then there was an old lady, or indeed I am not sure that she was as much old as antiquated and strangely out of place, who had left her husband, and was travelling all the way to Kansas by herself. We had to take her own word that she was married; for it was sorely contradicted by the testimony of her appearance. Nature seemed to have sanctified her for the single state; even the colour of her hair was incompatible with matrimony, and her husband, I thought, should be a man of saintly spirit and phantasmal bodily presence. She was ill, poor thing; her soul turned from the viands; the dirty tablecloth shocked her like an impropriety; and the whole strength of her endeavour was bent upon keeping her watch true to Glasgow time till she should reach New York. They had heard reports, her husband and she, of some unwarrantable disparity of hours between these two cities; and with a spirit commendably scientific, had seized on this occasion to put them to the proof. It was a good thing for the old lady; for she passed much leisure time in studying the watch. Once, when prostrated by sickness, she let it run down. It was inscribed on her harmless mind in letters of adamant that the hands of a watch must never be turned backwards;

and so it behoved her to lie in wait for the exact moment ere she started it again. When she imagined this was about due, she sought out one of the young second-cabin Scotsmen, who was embarked on the same experiment as herself and had hitherto been less neglectful. She was in quest of two o'clock; and when she learned it was already seven on the shores of Clyde, she lifted up her voice and cried 'Gravy!' I had not heard this innocent expletive since I was a young child; and I suppose it must have been the same with the other Scotsmen present, for we all laughed our fill.

Last but not least, I come to my excellent friend Mr. Jones. It would be difficult to say whether I was his right-hand man, or he mine, during the voyage. Thus at table I carved, while he only scooped gravy; but at our concerts, of which more anon, he was the president who called up performers to sing, and I but his messenger who ran his errands and pleaded privately with the over-modest. I knew I liked Mr. Jones from the moment I saw him. I thought him by his face to be Scottish; nor could his accent undeceive me. For as there is a lingua franca of many tongues on the moles and in the feluccas of the Mediterranean, so there is a free or common accent among English-speaking men who follow the sea. They catch a twang in a New England Port; from a cockney skipper, even a Scotsman sometimes learns to drop an h; a word of a dialect is picked up from another band in the forecastle; until often the result is undecipherable, and you have to ask for the man's place of birth. So it was with Mr. Jones. I thought him a Scotsman who had been long to sea; and yet he was from Wales, and had been most of his life a blacksmith at an inland forge; a few years in America and half a score of ocean voyages having sufficed to modify his speech into the common pattern. By his own account he was both strong and skilful in his trade. A few years back, he had been married and after a fashion a rich man; now the wife was dead and the money gone. But his was the nature that looks forward, and goes on from one year to another and through all the extremities of fortune undismayed; and if the sky were to fall to-morrow, I should look to see Jones, the day following, perched on a step-ladder and getting things to rights. He was always hovering round inventions like a bee over a flower, and lived in a dream of patents. He had with him a patent medicine, for instance, the composition of which he had bought years ago for five dollars from an American pedlar, and sold the other day for a hundred pounds (I think it was) to an English apothecary. It was called Golden Oil, cured all maladies without exception; and I am bound to say that I partook of it myself with good results.

It is a character of the man that he was not only perpetually dosing himself with Golden Oil, but wherever there was a head aching or a finger cut, there would be Jones with his bottle.

If he had one taste more strongly than another, it was to study character. Many an hour have we two walked upon the deck dissecting our neighbours in a spirit that was too purely scientific to be called unkind; whenever a quaint or human trait slipped out in conversation, you might have seen Jones and me exchanging glances; and we could hardly go to bed in comfort till we had exchanged notes and discussed the day's experience. We were then like a couple of anglers comparing a day's kill. But the fish we angled for were of a metaphysical species, and we angled as often as not in one another's baskets. Once, in the midst of a serious talk, each found there was a scrutinising eye upon himself; I own I paused in embarrassment at this double detection; but Jones, with a better civility, broke into a peal of unaffected laughter, and declared, what was the truth, that there was a pair of us indeed.

Early Impressions

We steamed out of the Clyde on Thursday night, and early on the Friday forenoon we took in our last batch of emigrants at Lough Foyle, in Ireland, and said farewell to Europe. The company was now complete, and began to draw together, by inscrutable magnetisms, upon the decks. There were Scots and Irish in plenty, a few English, a few Americans, a good handful of Scandinavians, a German or two, and one Russian; all now belonging for ten days to one small iron country on the deep.

As I walked the deck and looked round upon my fellow-passengers, thus curiously assorted from all northern Europe, I began for the first time to understand the nature of emigration. Day by day throughout the passage, and thenceforward across all the States, and on to the shores of the Pacific, this knowledge grew more clear and melancholy. Emigration, from a word of the most cheerful import, came to sound most dismally in my ear. There is nothing more agreeable to picture and nothing more pathetic to behold. The abstract idea, as conceived at home, is hopeful and adventurous. A young man, you fancy, scorning restraints and helpers, issues forth into life, that great battle, to fight for his own hand. The most pleasant stories of ambition, of difficulties overcome, and of ultimate success, are but as episodes to this great epic of self-help. The epic is composed of individual heroisms; it stands to them as the victorious war which subdued an empire stands to the personal act of bravery which spiked a single cannon and was adequately rewarded with a medal. For in emigration the young men enter direct and by the shipload on their heritage of work; empty continents swarm, as at the bo's'un's whistle, with industrious hands, and whole new empires are domesticated to the service of man.

This is the closet picture, and is found, on trial, to consist mostly of embellishments. The more I saw of my fellow-passengers, the less I was tempted to the lyric note. Comparatively few of the men were below thirty; many were married, and encumbered with families; not a few were already up in years; and this itself was out of tune with my imaginations, for the ideal emigrant should certainly be young. Again, I thought he should offer to the eye some bold type of humanity, with bluff or hawk-like features, and the stamp of an eager and pushing disposition. Now those around me were for the most part quiet, orderly, obedient citizens, family men broken by adversity, elderly youths who had failed to place themselves in life, and people who had seen better days. Mildness was the prevailing character; mild mirth and mild endurance. In a word, I was not taking part in an impetuous and conquering sally, such as swept over Mexico or Siberia, but found myself, like Marmion, 'in the lost battle, borne down by the flying.'

Labouring mankind had in the last years, and throughout Great Britain, sustained a prolonged and crushing series of defeats. I had heard vaguely of these reverses; of whole streets of houses standing deserted by the Tyne, the cellar-doors broken and removed for firewood; of homeless men loitering at the street-corners of Glasgow with their chests beside them; of closed factories, useless strikes, and starving girls. But I had never taken them home to me or represented these distresses livingly to my imagination.

A turn of the market may be a calamity as disastrous as the French retreat from Moscow; but it hardly lends itself to lively treatment, and makes a trifling figure in the morning papers. We may struggle as we please, we are not born economists. The individual is more affecting than the mass. It is by the scenic accidents, and the appeal to the carnal eye, that for the most part we grasp the significance of tragedies. Thus it was only now, when I found myself involved in the rout, that I began to appreciate how sharp had been the battle. We were a company of the rejected; the drunken, the incompetent, the weak, the prodigal, all who had been unable to prevail against circumstances in the one land, were now fleeing pitifully to another; and though one or two might still succeed, all had already failed. We were a shipful of failures, the broken men of England. Yet it must not be supposed that these people exhibited depression. The scene, on the contrary, was cheerful. Not a tear was shed on board the vessel. All were full of hope for the future, and showed an inclination to innocent gaiety. Some were heard to sing, and all began to scrape acquaintance with small jests and ready laughter.

The children found each other out like dogs, and ran about the decks scraping acquaintance after their fashion also. 'What do you call your mither?' I heard one ask. 'Mawmaw,' was the reply, indicating, I fancy, a shade of difference in the social scale. When people pass each other on the high seas of life at so early an age, the contact is but slight, and the relation more like what we may imagine to be the friendship of flies than that of men; it is so quickly joined, so easily dissolved, so open in its communications and so devoid of deeper human qualities. The children, I observed, were all in a band, and as thick as thieves at a fair, while their elders were still ceremoniously manoeuvring on the outskirts of acquaintance. The sea, the ship, and the seamen were soon as familiar as home to these half-conscious little ones. It was odd to hear them, throughout the voyage, employ shore words to designate portions of the vessel. 'Go 'way doon to yon dyke,' I heard one say, probably meaning the bulwark. I often had my heart in my mouth, watching them climb into the shrouds or on the rails, while the ship went swinging through the waves; and I admired and envied the courage of their mothers, who sat by in the sun and looked on with composure at these perilous feats. 'He'll maybe be a sailor,' I heard one remark; 'now's the time to learn.' I had been on the point of running forward to interfere, but stood back at that, reproved. Very few in the more delicate classes have the nerve to look upon the peril of one dear to them; but the life of poorer folk, where necessity is so much more immediate and imperious, braces even a mother to this extreme of endurance. And perhaps, after all, it is better that the lad should break his neck than that you should break his spirit.

And since I am here on the chapter of the children, I must mention one little fellow, whose family belonged to Steerage No. 4 and 5, and who, wherever he went, was like a strain of music round the ship. He was an ugly, merry, unbreeched child of three, his lint-white hair in a tangle, his face smeared with suet and treacle; but he ran to and fro with so natural a step, and fell and picked himself up again with such grace and good-humour, that he might fairly be called beautiful when he was in motion. To meet him, crowing with laughter and beating an accompaniment to his own mirth with a tin spoon upon a tin cup, was to meet a little triumph of the human species. Even when his mother and the rest of his family lay sick and prostrate around him, he sat upright in their midst and sang aloud in the pleasant heartlessness of infancy.

Throughout the Friday, intimacy among us men made but a few advances. We discussed the probable duration of the voyage, we exchanged pieces of information, naming our trades, what we hoped to find in the new world, or what we were fleeing from in the old; and, above all, we condoled together over the food and the vileness of the steerage. One or two had been so near famine that you may say they had run into the ship with the devil at their heels; and to these all seemed for the best in the best of possible steamers. But the majority were hugely contented. Coming as they did from a country in so low a state as Great Britain, many of them from Glasgow, which commercially speaking was as good as dead, and many having long been out of work, I was surprised to find them so dainty in their notions. I myself lived almost exclusively on bread, porridge, and soup, precisely as it was supplied to them, and found it, if not luxurious, at least sufficient. But these working men were loud in their outcries. It was not 'food for human beings,' it was 'only fit for pigs,' it was 'a disgrace.' Many of them lived almost entirely upon biscuit, others on their own private supplies, and some paid extra for better rations from the ship. This marvellously changed my notion of the degree of luxury habitual to the artisan. I was prepared to hear him grumble, for grumbling is the traveller's pastime; but I was not prepared to find him turn away from a diet which was palatable to myself. Words I should have disregarded, or taken with a liberal allowance; but when a man prefers dry biscuit there can be no question of the sincerity of his disgust.

With one of their complaints I could most heartily sympathise. A single night of the steerage had filled them with horror. I had myself suffered, even in my decent-second-cabin berth, from the lack of air; and as the night promised to be fine and quiet, I determined to sleep on deck, and advised all who complained of their quarters to follow my example. I dare say a dozen of others agreed to do so, and I thought we should have been quite a party. Yet, when I brought up my rug about seven bells, there was no one to be seen but the watch. That chimerical terror of good night-air, which makes men close their windows, list their doors, and seal themselves up with their own poisonous exhalations, had sent all these healthy workmen down below. One would think we had been brought up in a fever country; yet in England the most malarious districts are in the bedchambers.

I felt saddened at this defection, and yet half-pleased to have the night so quietly to myself. The wind had hauled a little ahead on the starboard bow, and was dry but chilly. I found a shelter near the fire-hole, and made myself snug for the night.

The ship moved over the uneven sea with a gentle and cradling movement. The ponderous, organic labours of the engine in her bowels occupied the mind, and prepared it for slumber. From time to time a heavier lurch would disturb me as I lay, and recall me to the obscure borders of consciousness; or I heard, as it were through a veil, the clear note of the clapper on the brass and the beautiful sea-cry, 'All's well!' I know nothing, whether for poetry or music, that can surpass the effect of these two syllables in the darkness of a night at sea.

The day dawned fairly enough, and during the early part we had some pleasant hours to improve acquaintance in the open air; but towards nightfall the wind freshened, the rain began to fall, and the sea rose so high that it was difficult to keep ones footing on the deck. I have spoken of our concerts. We were indeed a musical ship's company, and cheered our way into exile with the fiddle, the accordion, and the songs of all nations. Good, bad, or indifferent—Scottish, English, Irish, Russian, German or Norse,—the songs were received with generous applause. Once or twice, a recitation, very spiritedly rendered in a powerful Scottish accent, varied the proceedings; and once we sought in vain to dance a quadrille, eight men of us together, to the music of the violin. The performers were all humorous, frisky fellows, who loved to cut capers in private life; but as soon as they were arranged for the dance, they conducted themselves like so many mutes at a funeral. I have never seen decorum pushed so far; and as this was not expected, the quadrille was soon whistled down, and the dancers departed under a cloud. Eight Frenchmen, even eight Englishmen from another rank of society, would have dared to make some fun for themselves and the spectators; but the working man, when sober, takes an extreme and even melancholy view of personal deportment. A fifth-form schoolboy is not more careful of dignity. He dares not be comical; his fun must escape from him unprepared, and above all, it must be unaccompanied by any physical demonstration. I like his society under most circumstances, but let me never again join with him in public gambols.

But the impulse to sing was strong, and triumphed over modesty and even the inclemencies of sea and sky. On this rough Saturday night, we got together by the main deck-house, in a place sheltered from the wind and rain. Some clinging to a ladder which led to the hurricane deck, and the rest knitting arms or taking hands, we made a ring to support the women in the violent lurching of the ship; and when we were thus disposed, sang to our hearts' content. Some of the songs were appropriate to the scene; others strikingly the reverse. Bastard doggrel of the music-hall, such as, 'Around her splendid form, I weaved the magic circle,' sounded bald, bleak, and pitifully silly. 'We don't want to fight, but, by Jingo, if we do,' was in some measure saved by the vigour and unanimity with which the chorus was thrown forth into the night. I observed a Platt-Deutsch mason, entirely innocent of English, adding heartily to the general effect. And perhaps the German mason is but a fair example of the sincerity with which the song was rendered; for nearly all with whom I conversed upon the subject were bitterly opposed to war, and attributed their own misfortunes, and frequently their own taste for whisky, to the campaigns in Zululand and Afghanistan.

Every now and again, however, some song that touched the pathos of our situation was given forth; and you could hear by the voices that took up the burden how the sentiment came home to each, 'The Anchor's Weighed' was true for us. We were indeed 'Rocked on the bosom of the stormy deep.' How many of us could say with the singer, 'I'm lonely to-night, love, without you,' or, 'Go, some one, and tell them from me, to write me a letter from home'! And when was there a more appropriate moment for 'Auld Lang Syne' than now, when the land, the friends, and the affections of that mingled but beloved time were fading and fleeing behind us in the vessel's wake? It pointed forward to the hour when these labours should be overpast, to the return voyage, and to many a meeting in the sanded inn, when those who had parted in the spring of youth should again drink a cup of kindness in their age. Had not Burns contemplated emigration, I scarce believe he would have found that note.

All Sunday the weather remained wild and cloudy; many were prostrated by sickness; only five sat down to tea in the second cabin, and two of these departed abruptly ere the meal was at an end. The Sabbath was observed strictly by the majority of the emigrants. I heard an old woman express her surprise that 'the ship didna gae doon,' as she saw some one pass her with a chess-board on the holy day. Some sang Scottish psalms. Many went to service, and in true Scottish fashion came back ill pleased with their divine. 'I didna think he was an experienced preacher,' said one girl to me.

Is was a bleak, uncomfortable day; but at night, by six bells, although the wind had not yet moderated, the clouds were all wrecked and blown away behind the rim of the horizon, and the stars came out thickly overhead. I saw Venus burning as steadily and sweetly across this hurly-burly of the winds and waters as ever at home upon the summer woods. The engine pounded, the screw tossed out of the water with a roar, and shook the ship from end to end; the bows battled with loud reports against the billows: and as I stood in the lee-scuppers and looked up to where the funnel leaned out, over my head, vomiting smoke, and the black and monstrous top-sails blotted, at each lurch, a different crop of stars, it seemed as if all this trouble were a thing of small account, and that just above the mast reigned peace unbroken and eternal.

Steerage Scenes

Our companion (Steerage No. 2 and 3) was a favourite resort. Down one flight of stairs there was a comparatively large open space, the centre occupied by a hatchway, which made a convenient seat for about twenty persons, while barrels, coils of rope, and the carpenter's bench afforded perches for perhaps as many more. The canteen, or steerage bar, was on one side of the stair; on the other, a no less attractive spot, the cabin of the indefatigable interpreter.

I have seen people packed into this space like herrings in a barrel, and many merry evenings prolonged there until five bells, when the lights were ruthlessly extinguished and all must go to roost.

It had been rumoured since Friday that there was a fiddler aboard, who lay sick and unmelodious in Steerage No. 1; and on the Monday forenoon, as I came down the companion, I was saluted by something in Strathspey time. A white-faced Orpheus was cheerily playing to an audience of white-faced women. It was as much as he could do to play, and some of his hearers were scarce able to sit; yet they had crawled from their bunks at the first experimental flourish, and found better than medicine in the music. Some of the heaviest heads began to nod in time, and a degree of animation looked from some of the palest eyes. Humanly speaking, it is a more important matter to play the fiddle, even badly, than to write huge works upon recondite subjects. What could Mr. Darwin have done for these sick women? But this fellow scraped away; and the world was positively a better place for all who heard him. We have yet to understand the economical value of these mere accomplishments. I told the fiddler he was a happy man, carrying happiness about with him in his fiddle-case, and he seemed alive to the fact.

'It is a privilege,' I said. He thought a while upon the word, turning it over in his Scots head, and then answered with conviction, 'Yes, a privilege.'

That night I was summoned by 'Merrily danced the Quake's wife' into the companion of Steerage No. 4 and 5. This was, properly speaking, but a strip across a deck-house, lit by a sickly lantern which swung to and fro with the motion of the ship. Through the open slide-door we had a glimpse of a grey night sea, with patches of phosphorescent foam flying, swift as birds, into the wake, and the horizon rising and falling as the vessel rolled to the wind. In the centre the companion ladder plunged down sheerly like an open pit. Below, on the first landing, and lighted by another lamp, lads and lasses danced, not more than three at a time for lack of space, in jigs and reels and hornpipes. Above, on either side, there was a recess railed with iron, perhaps two feet wide and four long, which stood for orchestra and seats of honour. In the one balcony, five slatternly Irish lasses sat woven in a comely group. In the other was posted Orpheus, his body, which was convulsively in motion, forming an odd contrast to his somnolent, imperturbable Scots face. His brother, a dark man with a vehement, interested countenance, who made a god of the fiddler, sat by with open mouth, drinking in the general admiration and throwing out remarks to kindle it.

'That's a bonny hornpipe now,' he would say, 'it's a great favourite with performers; they dance the sand dance to it.' And he expounded the sand dance. Then suddenly, it would be a long, 'Hush!' with uplifted finger and glowing, supplicating eyes, 'he's going to play "Auld Robin Gray" on one string!' And throughout this excruciating movement,—'On one string, that's on one string!' he kept crying. I would have given something myself that it had been on none; but the hearers were much awed. I called for a tune or two, and thus introduced myself to the notice of the brother, who directed his talk to me for some little while, keeping, I need hardly mention, true to his topic, like the seamen to the star. 'He's grand of it,' he said confidentially. 'His master was a music-hall man.' Indeed the music-hall man had left his mark, for our fiddler was ignorant of many of our best old airs; 'Logie o' Buchan,' for instance, he only knew as a quick, jigging figure in a set of quadrilles, and had never heard it called by name. Perhaps, after all, the brother was the more interesting performer of the two. I have spoken with him afterwards repeatedly, and found him always the same quick, fiery bit of a man, not without brains; but he never showed to such advantage as when he was thus squiring the fiddler into public note. There is nothing more becoming than a genuine admiration; and it shares this with love, that it does not become contemptible although misplaced.

The dancing was but feebly carried on. The space was almost impracticably small; and the Irish wenches combined the extreme of bashfulness about this innocent display with a surprising impudence and roughness of address. Most often, either the fiddle lifted up its voice unheeded, or only a couple of lads would be footing it and snapping fingers on the landing. And such was the eagerness of the brother to display all the acquirements of his idol, and such the sleepy indifference of the performer, that the tune would as often as not be changed, and the hornpipe expire into a ballad before the dancers had cut half a dozen shuffles.

In the meantime, however, the audience had been growing more and more numerous every moment; there was hardly standing-room round the top of the companion; and the strange instinct of the race moved some of the newcomers to close both the doors, so that the atmosphere grew insupportable. It was a good place, as the saying is, to leave.

The wind hauled ahead with a head sea. By ten at night heavy sprays were flying and drumming over the forecastle; the companion of Steerage No. 1 had to be closed, and the door of communication through the second cabin thrown open. Either from the convenience of the opportunity, or because we had already a number of acquaintances in that part of the ship, Mr. Jones and I paid it a late visit. Steerage No. 1 is shaped like an isosceles triangle, the sides opposite the equal angles bulging outward with the contour of the ship. It is lined with eight pens of sixteen bunks apiece, four bunks below and four above on either side. At night the place is lit with two lanterns, one to each table. As the steamer beat on her way among the rough billows, the light passed through violent phases of change, and was thrown to and fro and up and down with startling swiftness. You were tempted to wonder, as you looked, how so thin a glimmer could control and disperse such solid blackness. When Jones and I entered we found a little company of our acquaintances seated together at the triangular foremost table. A more forlorn party, in more dismal circumstances, it would be hard to imagine. The motion here in the ship's nose was very violent; the uproar of the sea often overpoweringly loud. The yellow flicker of the lantern spun round and round and tossed the shadows in masses. The air was hot, but it struck a chill from its foetor.

From all round in the dark bunks, the scarcely human noises of the sick joined into a kind of farmyard chorus. In the midst, these five friends of mine were keeping up what heart they could in company. Singing was their refuge from discomfortable thoughts and sensations. One piped, in feeble tones, 'Oh why left I my hame?' which seemed a pertinent question in the circumstances. Another, from the invisible horrors of a pen where he lay dog-sick upon the upper-shelf, found courage, in a blink of his sufferings, to give us several verses of the 'Death of Nelson'; and it was odd and eerie to hear the chorus breathe feebly from all sorts of dark corners, and 'this day has done his dooty' rise and fall and be taken up again in this dim inferno, to an accompaniment of plunging, hollow-sounding bows and the rattling spray-showers overhead.

All seemed unfit for conversation; a certain dizziness had interrupted the activity of their minds; and except to sing they were tongue-tied. There was present, however, one tall, powerful fellow of doubtful nationality, being neither quite Scotsman nor altogether Irish, but of surprising clearness of conviction on the highest problems. He had gone nearly beside himself on the Sunday, because of a general backwardness to indorse his definition of mind as 'a living, thinking substance which cannot be felt, heard, or seen'—nor, I presume, although he failed to mention it, smelt. Now he came forward in a pause with another contribution to our culture.

'Just by way of change,' said he, 'I'll ask you a Scripture riddle. There's profit in them too,' he added ungrammatically.

This was the riddle—

C and P
Did agree
To cut down C;
But C and P
Could not agree
Without the leave of G;
All the people cried to see
The crueltie
Of C and P.

Harsh are the words of Mercury after the songs of Apollo! We were a long while over the problem, shaking our heads and gloomily wondering how a man could be such a fool; but at length he put us out of suspense and divulged the fact that C and P stood for Caiaphas and Pontius Pilate.

I think it must have been the riddle that settled us; but the motion and the close air likewise hurried our departure. We had not been gone long, we heard next morning, ere two or even three out of the five fell sick. We thought it little wonder on the whole, for the sea kept contrary all night. I now made my bed upon the second cabin floor, where, although I ran the risk of being stepped upon, I had a free current of air, more or less vitiated indeed, and running only from steerage to steerage, but at least not stagnant; and from this couch, as well as the usual sounds of a rough night at sea, the hateful coughing and retching of the sick and the sobs of children, I heard a man run wild with terror beseeching his friend for encouragement. 'The ship 's going down!' he cried with a thrill of agony. 'The ship's going down!' he repeated, now in a blank whisper, now with his voice rising towards a sob; and his friend might reassure him, reason with him, joke at him—all was in vain, and the old cry came back, 'The ship's going down!' There was something panicky and catching in the emotion of his tones; and I saw in a clear flash what an involved and hideous tragedy was a disaster to an emigrant ship. If this whole parishful of people came no more to land, into how many houses would the newspaper carry woe, and what a great part of the web of our corporate human life would be rent across for ever!

The next morning when I came on deck I found a new world indeed. The wind was fair; the sun mounted into a cloudless heaven; through great dark blue seas the ship cut a swath of curded foam. The horizon was dotted all day with companionable sails, and the sun shone pleasantly on the long, heaving deck.

We had many fine-weather diversions to beguile the time. There was a single chess-board and a single pack of cards. Sometimes as many as twenty of us would be playing dominoes for love. Feats of dexterity, puzzles for the intelligence, some arithmetical, some of the same order as the old problem of the fox and goose and cabbage, were always welcome; and the latter, I observed, more popular as well as more conspicuously well done than the former. We had a regular daily competition to guess the vessel's progress; and twelve o'clock, when the result was published in the wheel-house, came to be a moment of considerable interest. But the interest was unmixed. Not a bet was laid upon our guesses. From the Clyde to Sandy Hook I never heard a wager offered or taken. We had, besides, romps in plenty. Puss in the Corner, which we had rebaptized, in more manly style, Devil and four Corners, was my own favourite game; but there were many who preferred another, the humour of which was to box a person's ears until he found out who had cuffed him.

This Tuesday morning we were all delighted with the change of weather, and in the highest possible spirits. We got in a cluster like bees, sitting between each other's feet under lee of the deck-houses. Stories and laughter went around. The children climbed about the shrouds. White faces appeared for the first time, and began to take on colour from the wind. I was kept hard at work making cigarettes for one amateur after another, and my less than moderate skill was heartily admired. Lastly, down sat the fiddler in our midst and began to discourse his reels, and jigs, and ballads, with now and then a voice or two to take up the air and throw in the interest of human speech.

Through this merry and good-hearted scene there came three cabin passengers, a gentleman and two young ladies, picking their way with little gracious titters of indulgence, and a Lady-Bountiful air about nothing, which galled me to the quick. I have little of the radical in social questions, and have always nourished an idea that one person was as good as another. But I began to be troubled by this episode. It was astonishing what insults these people managed to convey by their presence. They seemed to throw their clothes in our faces. Their eyes searched us all over for tatters and incongruities. A laugh was ready at their lips; but they were too well-mannered to indulge it in our hearing. Wait a bit, till they were all back in the saloon, and then hear how wittily they would depict the manners of the steerage. We were in truth very innocently, cheerfully, and sensibly engaged, and there was no shadow of excuse for the swaying elegant superiority with which these damsels passed among us, or for the stiff and waggish glances of their squire. Not a word was said; only when they were gone Mackay sullenly damned their impudence under his breath; but we were all conscious of an icy influence and a dead break in the course of our enjoyment.

Steerage Types

We had a fellow on board, an Irish-American, for all the world like a beggar in a print by Callot; one-eyed, with great, splay crow's-feet round the sockets; a knotty squab nose coming down over his moustache; a miraculous hat; a shirt that had been white, ay, ages long ago; an alpaca coat in its last sleeves; and, without hyperbole, no buttons to his trousers. Even in these rags and tatters, the man twinkled all over with impudence like a piece of sham jewellery; and I have heard him offer a situation to one of his fellow-passengers with the air of a lord. Nothing could overlie such a fellow; a kind of base success was written on his brow. He was then in his ill days; but I can imagine him in

Congress with his mouth full of bombast and sawder. As we moved in the same circle, I was brought necessarily into his society. I do not think I ever heard him say anything that was true, kind, or interesting; but there was entertainment in the man's demeanour. You might call him a half-educated Irish Tigg.

Our Russian made a remarkable contrast to this impossible fellow. Rumours and legends were current in the steerages about his antecedents. Some said he was a Nihilist escaping; others set him down for a harmless spendthrift, who had squandered fifty thousand roubles, and whose father had now despatched him to America by way of penance. Either tale might flourish in security; there was no contradiction to be feared, for the hero spoke not one word of English. I got on with him lumberingly enough in broken German, and learned from his own lips that he had been an apothecary. He carried the photograph of his betrothed in a pocket-book, and remarked that it did not do her justice. The cut of his head stood out from among the passengers with an air of startling strangeness. The first natural instinct was to take him for a desperado; but although the features, to our Western eyes, had a barbaric and unhomely cast, the eye both reassured and touched. It was large and very dark and soft, with an expression of dumb endurance, as if it had often looked on desperate circumstances and never looked on them without resolution.

He cried out when I used the word. 'No, no,' he said, 'not resolution.'

'The resolution to endure,' I explained.

And then he shrugged his shoulders, and said, 'Ach, ja,' with gusto, like a man who has been flattered in his favourite pretensions. Indeed, he was always hinting at some secret sorrow; and his life, he said, had been one of unusual trouble and anxiety; so the legends of the steerage may have represented at least some shadow of the truth. Once, and once only, he sang a song at our concerts; standing forth without embarrassment, his great stature somewhat humped, his long arms frequently extended, his Kalmuck head thrown backward. It was a suitable piece of music, as deep as a cow's bellow and wild like the White Sea. He was struck and charmed by the freedom and sociality of our manners. At home, he said, no one on a journey would speak to him, but those with whom he would not care to speak; thus unconsciously involving himself in the condemnation of his countrymen. But Russia was soon to be changed; the ice of the Neva was softening under the sun of civilisation; the new ideas, 'wie eine feine Violine,' were audible among the big empty drum notes of Imperial diplomacy; and he looked to see a great revival, though with a somewhat indistinct and childish hope.

We had a father and son who made a pair of Jacks-of-all-trades. It was the son who sang the 'Death of Nelson' under such contrarious circumstances. He was by trade a shearer of ship plates; but he could touch the organ, and led two choirs, and played the flute and piccolo in a professional string band. His repertory of songs was, besides, inexhaustible, and ranged impartially from the very best to the very worst within his reach. Nor did he seem to make the least distinction between these extremes, but would cheerily follow up 'Tom Bowling' with 'Around her splendid form.'

The father, an old, cheery, small piece of man-hood, could do everything connected with tinwork from one end of the process to the other, use almost every carpenter's tool, and make picture frames to boot. 'I sat down with silver plate every Sunday,' said he, 'and pictures on the wall. I have made enough money to be rolling in my carriage. But, sir,' looking at me unsteadily with his bright rheumy eyes, 'I was troubled with a drunken wife.' He took a hostile view of matrimony in consequence. 'It's an old saying,' he remarked: 'God made 'em, and the devil he mixed 'em.'

I think he was justified by his experience. It was a dreary story. He would bring home three pounds on Saturday, and on Monday all the clothes would be in pawn. Sick of the useless struggle, he gave up a paying contract, and contented himself with small and ill-paid jobs. 'A bad job was as good as a good job for me,' he said; 'it all went the same way.' Once the wife showed signs of amendment; she kept steady for weeks on end; it was again worth while to labour and to do one's best. The husband found a good situation some distance from home, and, to make a little upon every hand, started the wife in a cook-shop; the children were here and there, busy as mice; savings began to grow together in the bank, and the golden age of hope had returned again to that unhappy family. But one week my old acquaintance, getting earlier through with his work, came home on the Friday instead of the Saturday, and there was his wife to receive him reeling drunk. He 'took and gave her a pair o' black eyes,' for which I pardon him, nailed up the cook-shop door, gave up his situation, and resigned himself to a life of poverty, with the workhouse at the end. As the children came to their full age they fled the house, and established themselves in other countries; some did well, some not so well; but the father remained at home alone with his drunken wife, all his sound-hearted pluck and varied accomplishments depressed and negatived.

Was she dead now? or, after all these years, had he broken the chain, and run from home like a schoolboy? I could not discover which; but here at least he was out on the adventure, and still one of the bravest and most youthful men on board.

'Now, I suppose, I must put my old bones to work again,' said he; 'but I can do a turn yet.'

And the son to whom he was going, I asked, was he not able to support him?

'Oh yes,' he replied. 'But I'm never happy without a job on hand. And I'm stout; I can eat a'most anything. You see no craze about me.'

This tale of a drunken wife was paralleled on board by another of a drunken father. He was a capable man, with a good chance in life; but he had drunk up two thriving businesses like a bottle of sherry, and involved his sons along with him in ruin. Now they were on board with us, fleeing his disastrous neighbourhood.

Total abstinence, like all ascetical conclusions, is unfriendly to the most generous, cheerful, and human parts of man; but it could have adduced many instances and arguments from among our ship's company. I was, one day conversing with a kind and happy Scotsman, running to fat and perspiration in the physical, but with a taste for poetry and a genial sense of fun. I had asked him his hopes in emigrating. They were like those of so many others, vague and unfounded; times were bad at home; they were said to have a turn for the better in the States; a man could get on anywhere, he thought. That was precisely the weak point of his position; for if he could get on in America, why could he not do the same in Scotland? But I never had the courage to use that argument, though it was often on the tip of my tongue, and instead I agreed with him heartily adding, with reckless originality, 'If the man stuck to his work, and kept away from drink.'

'Ah!' said he slowly, 'the drink! You see, that's just my trouble.'

He spoke with a simplicity that was touching, looking at me at the same time with something strange and timid in his eye, half-ashamed, half-sorry, like a good child who knows he should be beaten. You would have said he recognised a destiny to which he was born, and accepted the consequences mildly. Like the merchant Abudah, he was at the same time fleeing from his destiny and carrying it along with him, the whole at an expense of six guineas.

As far as I saw, drink, idleness, and incompetency were the three great causes of emigration, and for all of them, and drink first and foremost, this trick of getting transported overseas appears to me the silliest means of cure. You cannot run away from a weakness; you must some time fight it out or perish; and if that be so, why not now, and where you stand? Coelum non animam. Change Glenlivet for Bourbon, and it is still whisky, only not so good. A sea-voyage will not give a man the nerve to put aside cheap pleasure; emigration has to be done before we climb the vessel; an aim in life is the only fortune worth the finding; and it is not to be found in foreign lands, but in the heart itself.

Speaking generally, there is no vice of this kind more contemptible than another; for each is but a result and outward sign of a soul tragically ship-wrecked. In the majority of cases, cheap pleasure is resorted to by way of anodyne. The pleasure-seeker sets forth upon life with high and difficult ambitions; he meant to be nobly good and nobly happy, though at as little pains as possible to himself; and it is because all has failed in his celestial enterprise that you now behold him rolling in the garbage. Hence the comparative success of the teetotal pledge; because to a man who had nothing it sets at least a negative aim in life. Somewhat as prisoners beguile their days by taming a spider, the reformed drunkard makes an interest out of abstaining from intoxicating drinks, and may live for that negation. There is something, at least, *not to be done* each day; and a cold triumph awaits him every evening.

We had one on board with us, whom I have already referred to under the name Mackay, who seemed to me not only a good instance of this failure in life of which we have been speaking, but a good type of the intelligence which here surrounded me. Physically he was a small Scotsman, standing a little back as though he were already carrying the elements of a corporation, and his looks somewhat marred by the smallness of his eyes. Mentally, he was endowed above the average. There were but few subjects on which he could not converse with understanding and a dash of wit; delivering himself slowly and with gusto like a man who enjoyed his own sententiousness. He was a dry, quick, pertinent debater, speaking with a small voice, and swinging on his heels to launch and emphasise an argument. When he began a discussion, he could not bear to leave it off, but would pick the subject to the bone, without once relinquishing a point. An engineer by trade, Mackay believed in the unlimited perfectibility of all machines except the human machine. The latter he gave up with ridicule for a compound of carrion and perverse gases. He had an appetite for disconnected facts which I can only compare to the savage taste for beads. What is called information was indeed a passion with the man, and he not only delighted to receive it, but could pay you back in kind.

With all these capabilities, here was Mackay, already no longer young, on his way to a new country, with no prospects, no money, and but little hope. He was almost tedious in the cynical disclosures of his despair. 'The ship may go down for me,' he would say, 'now or to-morrow. I have nothing to lose and nothing to hope.' And again: 'I am sick of the whole damned performance.' He was, like the kind little man, already quoted, another so-called victim of the bottle. But Mackay was miles from publishing his weakness to the world; laid the blame of his failure on corrupt masters and a corrupt State policy; and after he had been one night overtaken and had played the buffoon in his cups, sternly, though not without tact, suppressed all reference to his escapade. It was a treat to see him manage this: the various jesters withered under his gaze, and you were forced to recognise in him a certain steely force, and a gift of command which might have ruled a senate.

In truth it was not whisky that had ruined him; he was ruined long before for all good human purposes but conversation. His eyes were sealed by a cheap, school-book materialism. He could see nothing in the world but money and steam-engines. He did not know what you meant by the word happiness. He had forgotten the simple emotions of childhood, and perhaps never encountered the delights of youth. He believed in production, that useful figment of economy, as if it had been real like laughter; and production, without prejudice to liquor, was his god and guide. One day he took me to task—novel cry to me—upon the over-payment of literature. Literary men, he said, were more highly paid than artisans; yet the artisan made threshing-machines and butter-churns, and the man of letters, except in the way of a few useful handbooks, made nothing worth the while. He produced a mere fancy article. Mackay's notion of a book was Hoppus's Measurer. Now in my time I have possessed and even studied that work; but if I were to be left to-morrow on Juan Fernandez, Hoppus's is not the book that I should choose for my companion volume.

I tried to fight the point with Mackay. I made him own that he had taken pleasure in reading books otherwise, to his view, insignificant; but he was too wary to advance a step beyond the admission. It was in vain for me to argue that here was pleasure ready-made and running from the spring, whereas his ploughs and butter-churns were but means and mechanisms to give men the necessary food and leisure before they start upon the search for pleasure; he jibbed and ran away from such conclusions. The thing was different, he declared, and nothing was serviceable but what had to do with food. 'Eat, eat, eat!' he cried; 'that's the bottom and the top.' By an odd irony of circumstance, he grew so much interested in this discussion that he let the hour slip by unnoticed and had to go without his tea. He had enough sense and humour, indeed he had no lack of either, to have chuckled over this himself in private; and even to me he referred to it with the shadow of a smile.

Mackay was a hot bigot. He would not hear of religion. I have seen him waste hours of time in argument with all sorts of poor human creatures who understood neither him nor themselves, and he had had the boyishness to dissect and criticise even so small a matter as the riddler's definition of mind. He snorted aloud with zealotry and the lust for intellectual battle. Anything, whatever it was, that seemed to him likely to discourage the continued passionate production of corn and steam-engines he resented like a conspiracy against the people. Thus, when I put in the plea for literature, that it was only in good books, or in the society of the good, that a man could get help in his conduct, he declared I was in a different world from him. 'Damn my conduct!' said he. 'I have given it up for a bad job. My question is, "Can I drive a nail?"' And he plainly looked upon me as one who was insidiously seeking to reduce the people's annual bellyful of corn and steam-engines.

It may be argued that these opinions spring from the defect of culture; that a narrow and pinching way of life not only exaggerates to a man the importance of material conditions, but indirectly, by denying him the necessary books and leisure, keeps his mind ignorant of larger thoughts; and that hence springs this overwhelming concern about diet, and hence the bald view of existence professed by Mackay. Had this been an English peasant the conclusion would be tenable. But Mackay had most of the elements of a liberal education. He had skirted metaphysical and mathematical studies. He had a thoughtful hold of what he knew, which would be exceptional among bankers. He had been brought up in the midst of hot-house piety, and told, with incongruous pride, the story of his own brother's deathbed ecstasies. Yet he had somehow failed to fulfil himself, and was adrift like a dead thing among external circumstances, without hope or lively preference or shaping aim. And further, there seemed a tendency among many of his fellows to fall into the same blank and unlovely opinions. One thing, indeed, is not to be learned in Scotland, and that is the way to be happy. Yet that is the whole of culture, and perhaps two-thirds of morality. Can it be that the Puritan school, by divorcing a man from nature, by thinning out his instincts, and setting a stamp of its disapproval on whole fields of human activity and interest, leads at last directly to material greed?

Nature is a good guide through life, and the love of simple pleasures next, if not superior, to virtue; and we had on board an Irishman who based his claim to the widest and most affectionate popularity precisely upon these two qualities, that he was natural and happy. He boasted a fresh colour, a tight little figure, unquenchable gaiety, and indefatigable goodwill. His clothes puzzled the diagnostic mind, until you heard he had been once a private coachman, when they became eloquent and seemed a part of his biography. His face contained the rest, and, I fear, a prophecy of the future; the hawk's nose above accorded so ill with the pink baby's mouth below. His spirit and his pride belonged, you might say, to the nose; while it was the general shiftlessness expressed by the other that had thrown him from situation to situation, and at length on board the emigrant ship. Barney ate, so to speak, nothing from the galley; his own tea, butter, and eggs supported him throughout the voyage; and about mealtime you might often find him up to the elbows in amateur cookery. His was the first voice heard singing among all the passengers; he was the first who fell to dancing. From Loch Foyle to Sandy Hook, there was not a piece of fun undertaken but there was Barney in the midst.

You ought to have seen him when he stood up to sing at our concerts—his tight little figure stepping to and fro, and his feet shuffling to the air, his eyes seeking and bestowing encouragement—and to have enjoyed the bow, so nicely calculated between jest and earnest, between grace and clumsiness, with which he brought each song to a conclusion. He was not only a great favourite among ourselves, but his songs attracted the lords of the saloon, who often leaned to hear him over the rails of the hurricane-deck. He was somewhat pleased, but not at all abashed, by this attention; and one night, in the midst of his famous performance of 'Billy Keogh,' I saw him spin half round in a pirouette and throw an audacious wink to an old gentleman above.

This was the more characteristic, as, for all his daffing, he was a modest and very polite little fellow among ourselves.

He would not have hurt the feelings of a fly, nor throughout the passage did he give a shadow of offence; yet he was always, by his innocent freedoms and love of fun, brought upon that narrow margin where politeness must be natural to walk without a fall. He was once seriously angry, and that in a grave, quiet manner, because they supplied no fish on Friday; for Barncy was a conscientious Catholic. He had likewise strict notions of refinement; and when, late one evening, after the women had retired, a young Scotsman struck up an indecent song, Barney's drab clothes were immediately missing from the group. His taste was for the society of gentlemen, of whom, with the reader's permission, there was no lack in our five steerages and second cabin; and he avoided the rough and positive with a girlish shrinking. Mackay, partly from his superior powers of mind, which rendered him incomprehensible, partly from his extreme opinions, was especially distasteful to the Irishman. I have seen him slink off with backward looks of terror and offended delicacy, while the other, in his witty, ugly way, had been professing hostility to God, and an extreme theatrical readiness to be shipwrecked on the spot. These utterances hurt the little coachman's modesty like a bad word.

The Sick Man

One night Jones, the young O'Reilly, and myself were walking arm-in-arm and briskly up and down the deck. Six bells had rung; a head-wind blew chill and fitful, the fog was closing in with a sprinkle of rain, and the fog-whistle had been turned on, and now divided time with its unwelcome outcries, loud like a bull, thrilling and intense like a mosquito. Even the watch lay somewhere snugly out of sight.

For some time we observed something lying black and huddled in the scuppers, which at last heaved a little and moaned aloud. We ran to the rails. An elderly man, but whether passenger or seaman it was impossible in the darkness to determine, lay grovelling on his belly in the wet scuppers, and kicking feebly with his outspread toes. We asked him what was amiss, and he replied incoherently, with a strange accent and in a voice unmanned by terror, that he had cramp in the stomach, that he had been ailing all day, had seen the doctor twice, and had walked the deck against fatigue till he was overmastered and had fallen where we found him.

Jones remained by his side, while O'Reilly and I hurried off to seek the doctor. We knocked in vain at the doctor's cabin; there came no reply; nor could we find any one to guide us. It was no time for delicacy; so we ran once more forward; and I, whipping up a ladder and touching my hat to the officer of the watch, addressed him as politely as I could—

'I beg your pardon, sir; but there is a man lying bad with cramp in the lee scuppers; and I can't find the doctor.'

He looked at me peeringly in the darkness; and then, somewhat harshly, 'Well, *I* can't leave the bridge, my man,' said he.

'No, sir; but you can tell me what to do,' I returned.

'Is it one of the crew?' he asked.

'I believe him to be a fireman,' I replied.

I dare say officers are much annoyed by complaints and alarmist information from their freight of human creatures; but certainly, whether it was the idea that the sick man was one of the crew, or from something conciliatory in my address, the officer in question was immediately relieved and mollified; and speaking in a voice much freer from constraint, advised me to find a steward and despatch him in quest of the doctor, who would now be in the smoking-room over his pipe.

One of the stewards was often enough to be found about this hour down our companion, Steerage No. 2 and 3; that was his smoking-room of a night. Let me call him Blackwood. O'Reilly and I rattled down the companion, breathing hurry; and in his shirt-sleeves and perched across the carpenters bench upon one thigh, found Blackwood; a neat, bright, dapper, Glasgow-looking man, with a bead of an eye and a rank twang in his speech. I forget who was with him, but the pair were enjoying a deliberate talk over their pipes. I dare say he was tired with his day's work, and eminently comfortable at that moment; and the truth is, I did not stop to consider his feelings, but told my story in a breath.

'Steward,' said I, 'there's a man lying bad with cramp, and I can't find the doctor.'

He turned upon me as pert as a sparrow, but with a black look that is the prerogative of man; and taking his pipe out of his mouth—

'That's none of my business,' said he. 'I don't care.'

I could have strangled the little ruffian where he sat. The thought of his cabin civility and cabin tips filled me with indignation. I glanced at O'Reilly; he was pale and quivering, and looked like assault and battery, every inch of him. But we had a better card than violence.

'You will have to make it your business,' said I, 'for I am sent to you by the officer on the bridge.'

Blackwood was fairly tripped. He made no answer, but put out his pipe, gave me one murderous look, and set off upon his errand strolling. From that day forward, I should say, he improved to me in courtesy, as though he had repented his evil speech and were anxious to leave a better impression.

When we got on deck again, Jones was still beside the sick man; and two or three late stragglers had gathered round, and were offering suggestions. One proposed to give the patient water, which was promptly negatived. Another bade us hold him up; he himself prayed to be let lie; but as it was at least as well to keep him off the streaming decks, O'Reilly and I supported him between us. It was only by main force that we did so, and neither an easy nor an agreeable duty; for he fought in his paroxysms like a frightened child, and moaned miserably when he resigned himself to our control.

'O let me lie!' he pleaded. 'I'll no' get better anyway.' And then, with a moan that went to my heart, 'O why did I come upon this miserable journey?'

I was reminded of the song which I had heard a little while before in the close, tossing steerage: 'O why left I my hame?'

Meantime Jones, relieved of his immediate charge, had gone off to the galley, where we could see a light. There he found a belated cook scouring pans by the radiance of two lanterns, and one of these he sought to borrow. The scullion was backward. 'Was it one of the crew?' he asked. And when Jones, smitten with my theory, had assured him that it was a fireman, he reluctantly left his scouring and came towards us at an easy pace, with one of the lanterns swinging from his finger. The light, as it reached the spot, showed us an elderly man, thick-set, and grizzled with years; but the shifting and coarse shadows concealed from us the expression and even the design of his face.

So soon as the cook set eyes on him he gave a sort of whistle.

'It's only a Passenger!' said he; and turning about, made, lantern and all, for the galley.

'He's a man anyway,' cried Jones in indignation.

'Nobody said he was a woman,' said a gruff voice, which I recognised for that of the bo's'un.

All this while there was no word of Blackwood or the doctor; and now the officer came to our side of the ship and asked, over the hurricane-deck rails, if the doctor were not yet come. We told him not.

'No?' he repeated with a breathing of anger; and we saw him hurry aft in person.

Ten minutes after the doctor made his appearance deliberately enough and examined our patient with the lantern. He made little of the case, had the man brought aft to the dispensary, dosed him, and sent him forward to his bunk. Two of his neighbours in the steerage had now come to our assistance, expressing loud sorrow that such 'a fine cheery body' should be sick; and these, claiming a sort of possession, took him entirely under their own care. The drug had probably relieved him, for he struggled no more, and was led along plaintive and patient, but protesting. His heart recoiled at the thought of the steerage. 'O let me lie down upon the bieldy side,' he cried; 'O dinna take me down!' And again: 'O why did ever I come upon this miserable voyage?' And yet once more, with a gasp and a wailing prolongation of the fourth word: 'I had no *call* to come.' But there he was; and by the doctor's orders and the kind force of his two shipmates disappeared down the companion of Steerage No.1 into the den allotted him.

At the foot of our own companion, just where I found Blackwood, Jones and the bo's'un were now engaged in talk. This last was a gruff, cruel-looking seaman, who must have passed near half a century upon the seas; square-headed, goat-bearded, with heavy blond eyebrows, and an eye without radiance, but inflexibly steady and hard. I had not forgotten his rough speech; but I remembered also that he had helped us about the lantern; and now seeing him in conversation with Jones, and being choked with indignation, I proceeded to blow off my steam.

'Well,' said I, 'I make you my compliments upon your steward,' and furiously narrated what had happened.

'I've nothing to do with him,' replied the bo's'un. 'They're all alike. They wouldn't mind if they saw you all lying dead one upon the top of another.'

This was enough. A very little humanity went a long way with me after the experience of the evening. A sympathy grew up at once between the bo's'un and myself; and that night, and during the next few days, I learned to appreciate him better. He was a remarkable type, and not at all the kind of man you find in books. He had been at Sebastopol under English colours; and again in a States ship, 'after the Alabama, and praying God we shouldn't find her.' He was a high Tory and a high Englishman. No manufacturer could have held opinions more hostile to the working man and his strikes. 'The workmen,' he said, 'think nothing of their country. They think of nothing but themselves. They're damned greedy, selfish fellows.' He would not hear of the decadence of England. 'They say they send us beef from America,' he argued; 'but who pays for it? All the money in the world's in England.' The Royal Navy was the best of possible services, according to him. 'Anyway the officers are gentlemen,' said he; 'and you can't get hazed to death by a damned non-commissioned—as you can in the army.' Among nations, England was the first; then came France. He respected the French navy and liked the French people; and if he were forced to make a new choice in life, 'by God, he would try Frenchmen!' For all his looks and rough, cold manners, I observed that children were never frightened by him; they divined him at once to be a friend; and one night when he had chalked his hand and clothes, it was incongruous to hear this formidable old salt chuckling over his boyish monkey trick.

In the morning, my first thought was of the sick man. I was afraid I should not recognise him, baffling had been the light of the lantern; and found myself unable to decide if he were Scots, English, or Irish. He had certainly employed north-country words and elisions; but the accent and the pronunciation seemed unfamiliar and incongruous in my ear.

To descend on an empty stomach into Steerage No. 1, was an adventure that required some nerve. The stench was atrocious; each respiration tasted in the throat like some horrible kind of cheese; and the squalid aspect of the place was aggravated by so many people worming themselves into their clothes in twilight of the bunks. You may guess if I was pleased, not only for him, but for myself also, when I heard that the sick man was better and had gone on deck.

The morning was raw and foggy, though the sun suffused the fog with pink and amber; the fog-horn still blew, stertorous and intermittent; and to add to the discomfort, the seamen were just beginning to wash down the decks. But for a sick man this was heaven compared to the steerage. I found him standing on the hot-water pipe, just forward of the saloon deck house. He was smaller than I had fancied, and plain-looking; but his face was distinguished by strange and fascinating eyes, limpid grey from a distance, but, when looked into, full of changing colours and grains of gold. His manners were mild and uncompromisingly plain; and I soon saw that, when once started, he delighted to talk. His accent and language had been formed in the most natural way, since he was born in Ireland, had lived a quarter of a century on the banks of Tyne, and was married to a Scots wife. A fisherman in the season, he had fished the east coast from Fisherrow to Whitby. When the season was over, and the great boats, which required extra hands, were once drawn up on shore till the next spring, he worked as a labourer about chemical furnaces, or along the wharves unloading vessels. In this comparatively humble way of life he had gathered a competence, and could speak of his comfortable house, his hayfield, and his garden. On this ship, where so many accomplished artisans were fleeing from starvation, he was present on a pleasure trip to visit a brother in New York.

Ere he started, he informed me, he had been warned against the steerage and the steerage fare, and recommended to bring with him a ham and tea and a spice loaf. But he laughed to scorn such counsels. 'I'm not afraid,' he had told his adviser; 'I'll get on for ten days. I've not been a fisherman for nothing.' For it is no light matter, as he reminded me, to be in an open boat, perhaps waist-deep with herrings, day breaking with a scowl, and for miles on every hand lee-shores, unbroken, iron-bound, surf-beat, with only here and there an anchorage where you dare not lie, or a harbour impossible to enter with the wind that blows. The life of a North Sea fisher is one long chapter of exposure and hard work and in-sufficient fare; and even if he makes land at some bleak fisher port, per-haps the season is bad or his boat has been unlucky and after fifty hours' unsleeping vigilance and toil, not a shop will give him credit for a loaf of bread. Yet the steerage of the emigrant ship had been too vile for the endurance of a man thus rudely trained. He had scarce eaten since he came on board, until the day before, when his appetite was tempted by some excellent pea-soup. We were all much of the same mind on board, and beginning with myself, had dined upon pea-soup not wisely but too well; only with him the excess had been punished, perhaps because he was weakened by former abstinence, and his first meal had resulted in a cramp. He had determined to live henceforth on biscuit; and when, two months later, he should return to England, to make the passage by saloon. The second cabin, after due inquiry, he scouted as another edi-tion of the steerage.

He spoke apologetically of his emotion when ill. 'Ye see, I had no call to be here,' said he; 'and I thought it was by with me last night. I've a good house at home, and plenty to nurse me, and I had no real call to leave them.' Speaking of the attentions he had received from his shipmates generally, 'they were all so kind,' he said, 'that there's none to mention.' And except in so far as I might share in this, he troubled me with no reference to my services.

But what affected me in the most lively manner was the wealth of this day-labourer, paying a two months' pleasure visit to the States, and preparing to return in the saloon, and the new testimony rendered by his story, not so much to the horrors of the steerage as to the habitual comfort of the working classes. One foggy, frosty December evening, I encountered on Liberton Hill, near Edinburgh, an Irish labourer trudg-ing homeward from the fields. Our roads lay together, and it was natural that we should fall into talk. He was covered with mud; an inoffensive, ignorant creature, who thought the Atlantic Cable was a secret con-trivance of the masters the better to oppress labouring mankind; and I confess I was astonished to learn that he had nearly three hundred pounds in the bank. But this man had travelled over most of the world, and enjoyed wonderful opportunities on some American railroad, with two dollars a shift and double pay on Sunday and at night; whereas my fellow-passenger had never quitted Tyneside, and had made all that he possessed in that same accursed, down-falling England, whence skilled mechanics, engineers, millwrights, and carpenters were fleeing as from the native country of starvation.

Fitly enough, we slid off on the subject of strikes and wages and hard times. Being from the Tyne, and a man who had gained and lost in his own pocket by these fluctuations, he had much to say, and held strong opinions on the subject. He spoke sharply of the masters, and, when I led him on, of the men also. The masters had been selfish and obstructive, the men selfish, silly, and light-headed. He rehearsed to me the course of a meeting at which he had been present, and the somewhat long discourse which he had there pronounced, calling into question the wisdom and even the good faith of the Union delegates; and although he had escaped himself through flush times and starvation times with a handsomely provided purse, he had so little faith in either man or master, and so profound a terror for the unerring Nemesis of mercantile affairs, that he could think of no hope for our country outside of a sudden and complete political subversion. Down must go Lords and Church and Army; and capital, by some happy direction, must change hands from worse to better, or England stood condemned. Such principles, he said, were growing 'like a seed.'

From this mild, soft, domestic man, these words sounded unusually ominous and grave. I had heard enough revolutionary talk among my workmen fellow-passengers; but most of it was hot and turgid, and fell discredited from the lips of unsuccessful men. This man was calm; he had attained prosperity and ease; he disapproved the policy which had been pursued by labour in the past; and yet this was his panacea,— to rend the old country from end to end, and from top to bottom, and in clamour and civil discord remodel it with the hand of violence.

The Stowaways

On the Sunday, among a party of men who were talking in our companion, Steerage No. 2 and 3, we remarked a new figure. He wore tweed clothes, well enough made if not very fresh, and a plain smoking-cap. His face was pale, with pale eyes, and spiritedly enough designed; but though not yet thirty, a sort of blackguardly degeneration had already overtaken his features. The fine nose had grown fleshy towards the point, the pale eyes were sunk in fat. His hands were strong and elegant; his experience of life evidently varied; his speech full of pith and verve; his manners forward, but perfectly presentable. The lad who helped in the second cabin told me, in answer to a question, that he did not know who he was, but thought, 'by his way of speaking, and because he was so polite, that he was some one from the saloon.'

I was not so sure, for to me there was something equivocal in his air and bearing. He might have been, I thought, the son of some good family who had fallen early into dissipation and run from home. But, making every allowance, how admirable was his talk! I wish you could have heard hin, tell his own stories. They were so swingingly set forth, in such dramatic language, and illustrated here and there by such luminous bits of acting, that they could only lose in any reproduction. There were tales of the P. and O. Company, where he had been an officer; of the East Indies, where in former years he had lived lavishly; of the Royal Engineers, where he had served for a period; and of a dozen other sides of life, each introducing some vigorous thumb-nail portrait. He had the talk to himself that night, we were all so glad to listen. The best talkers usually address themselves to some particular society; there they are kings, elsewhere camp-followers, as a man may know Russian and yet be ignorant of Spanish; but this fellow had a frank, headlong power of style, and a broad, human choice of subject, that would have turned any circle in the world into a circle of hearers. He was a Homeric talker, plain, strong, and cheerful; and the things and the people of which he spoke became readily and clearly present to the minds of those who heard him. This, with a certain added colouring of rhetoric and rodomontade, must have been the style of Burns, who equally charmed the ears of duchesses and hostlers.

Yet freely and personally as he spoke, many points remained obscure in his narration. The Engineers, for instance, was a service which he praised highly; it is true there would be trouble with the sergeants; but then the officers were gentlemen, and his own, in particular, one among ten thousand. It sounded so far exactly like an episode in the rakish, topsy-turvy life of such an one as I had imagined. But then there came incidents more doubtful, which showed an almost impudent greed after gratuities, and a truly impudent disregard for truth. And then there was the tale of his departure. He had wearied, it seems, of Woolwich, and one fine day, with a companion, slipped up to London for a spree. I have a suspicion that spree was meant to be a long one; but God disposes all things; and one morning, near Westminster Bridge, whom should he come across but the very sergeant who had recruited him at first! What followed? He himself indicated cavalierly that he had then resigned. Let us put it so. But these resignations are sometimes very trying.

At length, after having delighted us for hours, he took himself away from the companion; and I could ask Mackay who and what he was. 'That?' said Mackay. 'Why, that's one of the stowaways.'

'No man,' said the same authority, 'who has had anything to do with the sea, would ever think of paying for a passage.' I give the statement as Mackay's, without endorsement; yet I am tempted to believe that it contains a grain of truth; and if you add that the man shall be impudent and thievish, or else dead-broke, it may even pass for a fair representation of the facts. We gentlemen of England who live at home at ease have, I suspect, very insufficient ideas on the subject. All the world over, people are stowing away in coal-holes and dark corners, and when ships are once out to sea, appearing again, begrimed and bashful, upon deck. The career of these sea-tramps partakes largely of the adventurous. They may be poisoned by coal-gas, or die by starvation in their place of concealment; or when found they may be clapped at once and ignominiously into irons, thus to be carried to their promised land, the port of destination, and alas! brought back in the same way to that from which they started, and there delivered over to the magistrates and the seclusion of a county jail. Since I crossed the Atlantic, one miserable stowaway was found in a dying state among the fuel, uttered but a word or two, and departed for a farther country than America.

When the stowaway appears on deck, he has but one thing to pray for: that he be set to work, which is the price and sign of his forgiveness. After half an hour with a swab or a bucket, he feels himself as secure as if he had paid for his passage. It is not altogether a bad thing for the company, who get more or less efficient hands for nothing but a few plates of junk and duff; and every now and again find themselves better paid than by a whole family of cabin passengers. Not long ago, for instance, a packet was saved from nearly certain loss by the skill and courage of a stowaway engineer. As was no more than just, a handsome subscription rewarded him for his success: but even without such exceptional good fortune, as things stand in England and America, the stowaway will often make a good profit out of his adventure. Four engineers stowed away last summer on the same ship, the Circassia; and before two days after their arrival each of the four had found a comfortable berth. This was the most hopeful tale of emigration that I heard from first to last; and as you see, the luck was for stowaways.

My curiosity was much inflamed by what I heard; and the next morning, as I was making the round of the ship, I was delighted to find the ex-Royal Engineer engaged in washing down the white paint of a deck house. There was another fellow at work beside him, a lad not more than twenty, in the most miraculous tatters, his handsome face sown with grains of beauty and lighted up by expressive eyes. Four stowaways had been found aboard our ship before she left the Clyde, but these two had alone escaped the ignominy of being put ashore. Alick, my acquaintance of last night, was Scots by birth, and by trade a practical engineer; the other was from Devonshire, and had been to sea before the mast. Two people more unlike by training, character, and habits it would be hard to imagine; yet here they were together, scrubbing paint.

Alick had held all sorts of good situations, and wasted many opportunities in life. I have heard him end a story with these words: 'That was in my golden days, when I used finger-glasses.' Situation after situation failed him; then followed the depression of trade, and for months he had hung round with other idlers, playing marbles all day in the West Park, and going home at night to tell his landlady how he had been seeking for a job. I believe this kind of existence was not unpleasant to Alick himself, and he might have long continued to enjoy idleness and a life on tick; but he had a comrade, let us call him Brown, who grew restive. This fellow was continually threatening to slip his cable for the States, and at last, one Wednesday, Glasgow was left widowed of her Brown. Some months afterwards, Alick met another old chum in Sauchiehall Street.

'By the bye, Alick,' said he, 'I met a gentleman in New York who was asking for you.'

'Who was that?' asked Alick.

'The new second engineer on board the So-and-so,' was the reply.

'Well, and who is he?'

'Brown, to be sure.'

For Brown had been one of the fortunate quartette aboard the Circassia. If that was the way of it in the States, Alick thought it was high time to follow Brown's example. He spent his last day, as he put it, 'reviewing the yeomanry,' and the next morning says he to his landlady, 'Mrs. x., I'll not take porridge to-day, please; I'll take some eggs.'

'Why, have you found a job?' she asked, delighted.

'Well, yes,' returned the perfidious Alick; 'I think I'll start to-day.'

And so, well lined with eggs, start he did, but for America. I am afraid that landlady has seen the last of him.

It was easy enough to get on board in the confusion that attends a vessel's departure; and in one of the dark corners of Steerage No. 1, flat in a bunk and with an empty stomach, Alick made the voyage from the Broomielaw to Greenock. That night, the ship's yeoman pulled him out by the heels and had him before the mate. Two other stowaways had already been found and sent ashore; but by this time darkness had fallen, they were out in the middle of the estuary, and the last steamer had left them till the morning.

'Take him to the forecastle and give him a meal,' said the mate, 'and see and pack him off the first thing to-morrow.'

In the forecastle he had supper, a good night's rest, and breakfast; and was sitting placidly with a pipe, fancying all was over and the game up for good with that ship, when one of the sailors grumbled out an oath at him, with a 'What are you doing there?' and 'Do you call that hiding, anyway?' There was need of no more; Alick was in another bunk before the day was older. Shortly before the passengers arrived, the ship was cursorily inspected. He heard the round come down the companion and look into one pen after another, until they came within two of the one in which he lay concealed. Into these last two they did not enter, but merely glanced from without; and Alick had no doubt that he was personally favoured in this escape. It was the character of the man to attribute nothing to luck and but little to kindness; whatever happened to him he had earned in his own right amply; favours came to him from his singular attraction and adroitness, and misfortunes he had always accepted with his eyes open. Half an hour after the searchers had departed, the steerage began to fill with legitimate passengers, and the worst of Alick's troubles was at an end. He was soon making himself popular, smoking other people's tobacco, and politely sharing their private stock delicacies, and when night came he retired to his bunk beside the others with composure.

Next day by afternoon, Lough Foyle being already far behind, and only the rough north-western hills of Ireland within view, Alick appeared on deck to court inquiry and decide his fate. As a matter of fact, he was known to several on board, and even intimate with one of the engineers; but it was plainly not the etiquette of such occasions for the authorities to avow their information. Every one professed surprise and anger on his appearance, and he was led prison before the captain.

'What have you got to say for yourself?' inquired the captain.

'Not much,' said Alick; 'but when a man has been a long time out of a job, he will do things he would not under other circumstances.'

'Are you willing to work?'

Alick swore he was burning to be useful.

'And what can you do?' asked the captain.

He replied composedly that he was a brass-fitter by trade.

'I think you will be better at engineering?' suggested the officer, with a shrewd look.

'No, sir,' says Alick simply.—'There's few can beat me at a lie,' was his engaging commentary to me as he recounted the affair.

'Have you been to sea?' again asked the captain.

'I've had a trip on a Clyde steamboat, sir, but no more,' replied the unabashed Alick.

'Well, we must try and find some work for you,' concluded the officer.

And hence we behold Alick, clear of the hot engine-room, lazily scraping paint and now and then taking a pull upon a sheet. 'You leave me alone,' was his deduction. 'When I get talking to a man, I can get round him.'

The other stowaway, whom I will call the Devonian—it was noticeable that neither of them told his name—had both been brought up and seen the world in a much smaller way. His father, a confectioner, died and was closely followed by his mother. His sisters had taken, I think, to dressmaking. He himself had returned from sea about a year ago and gone to live with his brother, who kept the 'George Hotel'—'it was not quite a real hotel,' added the candid fellow—'and had a hired man to mind the horses.' At first the Devonian was very welcome; but as time went on his brother not unnaturally grew cool towards him, and he began to find himself one too many at the 'George Hotel.' 'I don't think brothers care much for you,' he said, as a general reflection upon life. Hurt at this change, nearly penniless, and too proud to ask for more, he set off on foot and walked eighty miles to Weymouth, living on the journey as he could. He would have enlisted, but he was too small for the army and too old for the navy; and thought himself fortunate at last to find a berth on board a trading dandy. Somewhere in the Bristol Channel the dandy sprung a leak and went down; and though the crew were picked up and brought ashore by fishermen, they found themselves with nothing but the clothes upon their back. His next engagement was scarcely better starred; for the ship proved so leaky, and frightened them all so heartily during a short passage through the Irish Sea, that the entire crew deserted and remained behind upon the quays of Belfast.

Evil days were now coming thick on the Devonian. He could find no berth in Belfast, and had to work a passage to Glasgow on a steamer. She reached the Broomielaw on a Wednesday: the Devonian had a bellyful that morning, laying in breakfast manfully to provide against the future, and set off along the quays to seek employment. But he was now not only penniless, his clothes had begun to fall in tatters; he had begun to have the look of a street Arab; and captains will have nothing to say to a ragamuffin; for in that trade, as in all others, it is the coat that depicts the man. You may hand, reef, and steer like an angel, but if you have a hole in your trousers, it is like a millstone round your neck. The Devonian lost heart at so many refusals. He had not the impudence to beg; although, as he said, 'when I had money of my own, I always gave it.' It was only on Saturday morning, after three whole days of starvation, that he asked a scone from a milkwoman, who added of her own accord a glass of milk. He had now made up his mind to stow away, not from any desire to see America, but merely to obtain the comfort of a place in the forecastle and a supply of familiar sea-fare. He lived by begging, always from milkwomen, and always scones and milk, and was not once refused. It was vile wet weather, and he could never have been dry. By night he walked the streets, and by day slept upon Glasgow Green, and heard, in the intervals of his dozing, the famous theologians of the spot clear up intricate points of doctrine and appraise the merits of the clergy. He had not much instruction; he could 'read bills on the street,' but was 'main bad at writing'; yet these theologians seem to have impressed him with a genuine sense of amusement. Why he did not go to the Sailors' House I know not; I presume there is in Glasgow one of these institutions, which are by far the happiest and the wisest effort of contemporaneous charity; but I must stand to my author, as they say in old books, and relate the story as I heard it. In the meantime, he had tried four times to stow away in different vessels, and four times had been discovered and handed back to starvation. The fifth time was lucky; and you may judge if he were pleased to be aboard ship again, at his old work, and with duff twice a week. He was, said Alick, 'a devil for the duff.' Or if devil was not the word, it was one if anything stronger.

The difference in the conduct of the two was remarkable. The Devonian was as willing as any paid hand, swarmed aloft among the first, pulled his natural weight and firmly upon a rope, and found work for himself when there was none to show him. Alick, on the other hand, was not only a skulker in the brain, but took a humorous and fine gentle-manly view of the transaction. He would speak to me by the hour in ostentatious idleness; and only if the bo's'un or a mate came by, fell-to languidly for just the necessary time till they were out of sight. 'I'm not breaking my heart with it,' he remarked.

Once there was a hatch to be opened near where he was stationed; he watched the preparations for a second or so suspiciously, and then, 'Hullo,' said he, 'here's some real work coming—I'm off,' and he was gone that moment. Again, calculating the six guinea passage-money, and the probable duration of the passage, he remarked pleasantly that he was getting six shillings a day for this job, 'and it's pretty dear to the company at that.' 'They are making nothing by me,' was another of his observations; 'they're making something by that fellow.' And he pointed to the Devonian, who was just then busy to the eyes.

The more you saw of Alick, the more, it must be owned, you learned to despise him. His natural talents were of no use either to himself or others; for his character had degenerated like his face, and become pulpy and pretentious. Even his power of persuasion, which was cer-tainly very surprising, stood in some danger of being lost or neutra-lised by over-confidence. He lied in an aggressive, brazen manner, like a pert criminal in the dock; and he was so vain of his own cleverness that he could not refrain from boasting, ten minutes after, of the very trick by which he had deceived you. 'Why, now I have more money than when I came on board,' he said one night, exhibiting a sixpence, 'and yet I stood myself a bottle of beer before I went to bed yesterday. And as for tobacco, I have fifteen sticks of it.' That was fairly successful indeed; yet a man of his superiority, and with a less obtrusive policy, might, who knows? have got the length of half a crown. A man who prides himself upon persuasion should learn the persuasive faculty of silence, above all as to his own misdeeds. It is only in the farce and for dramatic purposes that Scapin enlarges on his peculiar talents to the world at large.

Scapin is perhaps a good name for this clever, unfortunate Alick; for at the bottom of all his misconduct there was a guiding sense of humour that moved you to forgive him. It was more than half a jest that he conducted his existence. 'Oh, man,' he said to me once with unusual emotion, like a man thinking of his mistress, 'I would give up anything for a lark.'

It was in relation to his fellow-stowaway that Alick showed the best, or perhaps I should say the only good, points of his nature. 'Mind you,' he said suddenly, changing his tone, 'mind you that's a good boy. He wouldn't tell you a lie. A lot of them think he is a scamp because his clothes are ragged, but he isn't; he's as good as gold.' To hear him, you become aware that Alick himself had a taste for virtue. He thought his own idleness and the other's industry equally becoming. He was no more anxious to insure his own reputation as a liar than to uphold the truthfulness of his companion; and he seemed unaware of what was incongruous in his attitude, and was plainly sincere in both characters.

It was not surprising that he should take an interest in the Devonian, for the lad worshipped and served him in love and wonder. Busy as he was, he would find time to warn Alick of an approaching officer, or even to tell him that the coast was clear, and he might slip off and smoke a pipe in safety. 'Tom,' he once said to him, for that was the name which Alick ordered him to use, 'if you don't like going to the galley, I'll go for you. You ain't used to this kind of thing, you ain't. But I'm a sailor; and I can understand the feelings of any fellow, I can.' Again, he was hard up, and casting about for some tobacco, for he was not so liberally used in this respect as others perhaps less worthy, when Alick offered him the half of one of his fifteen sticks. I think, for my part, he might have increased the offer to a whole one, or perhaps a pair of them, and not lived to regret his liberality. But the Devonian refused. 'No,' he said, 'you're a stowaway like me; I won't take it from you, I'll take it from some one who's not down on his luck.'

It was notable in this generous lad that he was strongly under the influence of sex. If a woman passed near where he was working, his eyes lit up, his hand paused, and his mind wandered instantly to other thoughts. It was natural that he should exercise a fascination proportionally strong upon women. He begged, you will remember, from women only, and was never refused. Without wishing to explain away the charity of those who helped him, I cannot but fancy he may have owed a little to his handsome face, and to that quick, responsive nature, formed for love, which speaks eloquently through all disguises, and can stamp an impression in ten minutes' talk or an exchange of glances. He was the more dangerous in that he was far from bold, but seemed to woo in spite of himself, and with a soft and pleading eye. Ragged as he was, and many a scarecrow is in that respect more comfortably furnished, even on board he was not without some curious admirers.

There was a girl among the passengers, a tall, blonde, handsome, strapping Irishwoman, with a wild, accommodating eye, whom Alick had dubbed Tommy, with that transcendental appropriateness that defies analysis. One day the Devonian was lying for warmth in the upper stoke-hole, which stands open on the deck, when Irish Tommy came past, very neatly attired, as was her custom.

'Poor fellow,' she said, stopping, 'you haven't a vest.'

'No,' he said; 'I wish I 'ad.'

Then she stood and gazed on him in silence, until, in his embarrassment, for he knew not how to look under this scrutiny, he pulled out his pipe and began to fill it with tobacco.

'Do you want a match?' she asked. And before he had time to reply, she ran off and presently returned with more than one.

That was the beginning and the end, as far as our passage is concerned, of what I will make bold to call this love-affair. There are many relations which go on to marriage and last during a lifetime, in which less human feeling is engaged than in this scene of five minutes at the stoke-hole.

Rigidly speaking, this would end the chapter of the stowaways; but in a larger sense of the word I have yet more to add. Jones had discovered and pointed out to me a young woman who was remarkable among her fellows for a pleasing and interesting air. She was poorly clad, to the verge, if not over the line, of disrespectability, with a ragged old jacket and a bit of a sealskin cap no bigger than your fist; but her eyes, her whole expression, and her manner, even in ordinary moments, told of a true womanly nature, capable of love, anger, and devotion. She had a look, too, of refinement, like one who might have been a better lady than most, had she been allowed the opportunity. When alone she seemed preoccupied and sad; but she was not often alone; there was usually by her side a heavy, dull, gross man in rough clothes, chary of speech and gesture—not from caution, but poverty of disposition; a man like a ditcher, unlovely and uninteresting; whom she petted and tended and waited on with her eyes as if he had been Amadis of Gaul. It was strange to see this hulking fellow dog-sick, and this delicate, sad woman caring for him. He seemed, from first to last, insensible of her caresses and attentions, and she seemed unconscious of his insensibility. The Irish husband, who sang his wife to sleep, and this Scottish girl serving her Orson, were the two bits of human nature that most appealed to me throughout the voyage.

On the Thursday before we arrived, the tickets were collected; and soon a rumour began to go round the vessel; and this girl, with her bit of sealskin cap, became the centre of whispering and pointed fingers. She also, it was said, was a stowaway of a sort; for she was on board with neither ticket nor money; and the man with whom she travelled was the father of a family, who had left wife and children to be hers. The ship's officers discouraged the story, which may therefore have been a story and no more; but it was believed in the steerage, and the poor girl had to encounter many curious eyes from that day forth.

Personal Experience and Review

Travel is of two kinds; and this voyage of mine across the ocean combined both. 'Out of my country and myself I go,' sings the old poet: and I was not only travelling out of my country in latitude and longitude, but out of myself in diet, associates, and consideration. Part of the interest and a great deal of the amusement flowed, at least to me, from this novel situation in the world.

I found that I had what they call fallen in life with absolute success and verisimilitude. I was taken for a steerage passenger; no one seemed surprised that I should be so; and there was nothing but the brass plate between decks to remind me that I had once been a gentleman. In a former book, describing a former journey, I expressed some wonder that I could be readily and naturally taken for a pedlar, and explained the accident by the difference of language and manners between England and France. I must now take a humbler view; for here I was among my own countrymen, somewhat roughly clad to be sure, but with every advantage of speech and manner; and I am bound to confess that I passed for nearly anything you please except an educated gentleman. The sailors called me 'mate,' the officers addressed me as 'my man,' my comrades accepted me without hesitation for a person of their own character and experience, but with some curious information. One, a mason himself, believed I was a mason; several, and among these at least one of the seaman, judged me to be a petty officer in the American navy; and I was so often set down for a practical engineer that at last I had not the heart to deny it. From all these guesses I drew one conclusion, which told against the insight of my companions. They might be close observers in their own way, and read the manners in the face; but it was plain that they did not extend their observation to the hands.

To the saloon passengers also I sustained my part without a hitch. It is true I came little in their way; but when we did encounter, there was no recognition in their eye, although I confess I sometimes courted it in silence. All these, my inferiors and equals, took me, like the transformed monarch in the story, for a mere common, human man. They gave me a hard, dead look, with the flesh about the eye kept unrelaxed.

With the women this surprised me less, as I had already experimented on the sex by going abroad through a suburban part of London simply attired in a sleeve-waistcoat. The result was curious. I then learned for the first time, and by the exhaustive process, how much attention ladies are accustomed to bestow on all male creatures of their own station; for, in my humble rig, each one who went by me caused me a certain shock of surprise and a sense of something wanting. In my normal circumstances, it appeared every young lady must have paid me some tribute of a glance; and though I had often not detected it when it was given, I was well aware of its absence when it was withheld. My height seemed to decrease with every woman who passed me, for she passed me like a dog. This is one of my grounds for supposing that what are called the upper classes may sometimes produce a disagreeable impression in what are called the lower; and I wish some one would continue my experiment, and find out exactly at what stage of toilette a man becomes invisible to the well-regulated female eye.

Here on shipboard the matter was put to a more complete test; for, even with the addition of speech and manner, I passed among the ladies for precisely the average man of the steerage. It was one afternoon that I saw this demonstrated. A very plainly dressed woman was taken ill on deck. I think I had the luck to be present at every sudden seizure during all the passage; and on this occasion found myself in the place of importance, supporting the sufferer. There was not only a large crowd immediately around us, but a considerable knot of saloon passengers leaning over our heads from the hurricane-deck. One of these, an elderly managing woman, hailed me with counsels. Of course I had to reply; and as the talk went on, I began to discover that the whole group took me for the husband. I looked upon my new wife, poor creature, with mingled feelings; and I must own she had not even the appearance of the poorest class of city servant-maids, but looked more like a country wench who should have been employed at a roadside inn. Now was the time for me to go and study the brass plate.

To such of the officers as knew about me—the doctor, the purser, and the stewards—I appeared in the light of a broad joke. The fact that I spent the better part of my day in writing had gone abroad over the ship and tickled them all prodigiously. Whenever they met me they referred to my absurd occupation with familiarity and breadth of humorous intention. Their manner was well calculated to remind me of my fallen fortunes. You may be sincerely amused by the amateur literary efforts of a gentleman, but you scarce publish the feeling to his face. 'Well!' they would say: 'still writing?' And the smile would widen into a laugh. The purser came one day into the cabin, and, touched to the heart by my misguided industry, offered me some other kind of writing, 'for which,' he added pointedly, 'you will be paid.' This was nothing else than to copy out the list of passengers.

Another trick of mine which told against my reputation was my choice of roosting-place in an active draught upon the cabin floor. I was openly jeered and flouted for this eccentricity; and a considerable knot would sometimes gather at the door to see my last dispositions for the night. This was embarrassing, but I learned to support the trial with equanimity.

Indeed I may say that, upon the whole, my new position sat lightly and naturally upon my spirits. I accepted the consequences with readiness, and found them far from difficult to bear. The steerage conquered me; I conformed more and more to the type of the place, not only in manner but at heart, growing hostile to the officers and cabin passengers who looked down upon me, and day by day greedier for small delicacies. Such was the result, as I fancy, of a diet of bread and butter, soup and porridge. We think we have no sweet tooth as long as we are full to the brim of molasses; but a man must have sojourned in the workhouse before he boasts himself indifferent to dainties. Every evening, for instance, I was more and more preoccupied about our doubtful fare at tea. If it was delicate my heart was much lightened; if it was but broken fish I was proportionally downcast. The offer of a little jelly from a fellow-passenger more provident than myself caused a marked elevation in my spirits. And I would have gone to the ship's end and back again for an oyster or a chipped fruit.

In other ways I was content with my position. It seemed no disgrace to be confounded with my company; for I may as well declare at once I found their manners as gentle and becoming as those of any other class. I do not mean that my friends could have sat down without embarrassment and laughable disaster at the table of a duke. That does not imply an inferiority of breeding, but a difference of usage. Thus I flatter myself that I conducted myself well among my fellow-passengers; yet my most ambitious hope is not to have avoided faults, but to have committed as few as possible. I know too well that my tact is not the same as their tact, and that my habit of a different society constituted, not only no qualification, but a positive disability to move easily and becomingly in this. When Jones complimented me—because I 'managed to behave very pleasantly' to my fellow-passengers, was how he put it—I could follow the thought in his mind, and knew his compliment to be such as we pay foreigners on their proficiency in English. I dare say this praise was given me immediately on the back of some unpardonable sole- cism, which had led him to review my conduct as a whole. We are all ready to laugh at the ploughman among lords; we should consider also the case of a lord among the ploughmen. I have seen a lawyer in the house of a Hebridean fisherman; and I know, but nothing will induce me to disclose, which of these two was the better gentleman. Some of our finest behaviour, though it looks well enough from the boxes, may seem even brutal to the gallery. We boast too often manners that are parochial rather than universal; that, like a country wine, will not bear transportation for a hundred miles, nor from the parlour to the kitchen. To be a gentleman is to be one all the world over, and in every relation and grade of society. It is a high calling, to which a man must first be born, and then devote himself for life. And, unhappily, the manners of a certain so-called upper grade have a kind of currency, and meet with a certain external acceptation throughout all the others, and this tends to keep us well satisfied with slight acquirements and the amateurish accomplishments of a clique. But manners, like art, should be human and central.

Some of my fellow-passengers, as I now moved among them in a relation of equality, seemed to me excellent gentlemen. They were not rough, nor hasty, nor disputatious; debated pleasantly, differed kindly; were helpful, gentle, patient, and placid. The type of manners was plain, and even heavy; there was little to please the eye, but noth- ing to shock; and I thought gentleness lay more nearly at the spring of behaviour than in many more ornate and delicate societies. I say delicate, where I cannot say refined; a thing may be fine, like ironwork, without being delicate, like lace. There was here less delicacy; the skin supported more callously the natural surface of events, the mind re- ceived more bravely the crude facts of human existence; but I do not think that there was less effective refinement, less consideration for others, less polite suppression of self. I speak of the best among my fellow-passengers; for in the steerage, as well as in the saloon, there is a mixture. Those, then, with whom I found myself in sympathy, and of whom I may therefore hope to write with a greater measure of truth, were not only as good in their manners, but endowed with very much the same natural capacities, and about as wise in deduction, as the bankers and barristers of what is called society. One and all were too much interested in disconnected facts, and loved information for its own sake with too rash a devotion; but people in all classes display the same appetite as they gorge themselves daily with the miscellaneous gossip of the newspaper. Newspaper-reading, as far as I can make out, is often rather a sort of brown study than an act of culture. I have myself palmed off yesterday's issue on a friend, and seen him re-peruse it for a continuance of minutes with an air at once refreshed and solemn. Workmen, perhaps, pay more attention; but though they may be eager listeners, they have rarely seemed to me either willing or careful thinkers. Culture is not measured by the greatness of the field which is covered by our knowledge, but by the nicety with which we can perceive relations in that field, whether great or small. Workmen, certainly those who were on board with me, I found wanting in this quality or habit of the mind. They did not perceive relations, but leaped to a so-called cause, and thought the problem settled. Thus the cause of everything in England was the form of government, and the cure for all evils was, by consequence, a revolution. It is surprising how many of them said this, and that none should have had a definite thought in his head as he said it. Some hated the Church because they disagreed with it; some hated Lord Beaconsfield because of war and taxes; all hated the masters, possibly with reason. But these failings were not at the root of the matter; the true reasoning of their souls ran thus—I have not got on; I ought to have got on; if there was a revolution I should get on. How? They had no idea. Why? Because—because—well, look at America!

To be politically blind is no distinction; we are all so, if you come to that. At bottom, as it seems to me, there is but one question in modern home politics, though it appears in many shapes, and that is the question of money; and but one political remedy, that the people should grow wiser and better. My workmen fellow-passengers were as impatient and dull of hearing on the second of these points as any member of Parliament; but they had some glimmerings of the first. They would not hear of improvement on their part, but wished the world made over again in a crack, so that they might remain improvident and idle and debauched, and yet enjoy the comfort and respect that should accompany the opposite virtues; and it was in this expectation, as far as I could see, that many of them were now on their way to America. But on the point of money they saw clearly enough that inland politics, so far as they were concerned, were reducible to the question of annual income; a question which should long ago have been settled by a revolution, they did not know how, and which they were now about to settle for themselves, once more they knew not how, by crossing the Atlantic in a steamship of considerable tonnage.

And yet it has been amply shown them that the second or income question is in itself nothing, and may as well be left undecided, if there be no wisdom and virtue to profit by the change. It is not by a man's purse, but by his character that he is rich or poor. Barney will be poor, Alick will be poor, Mackay will be poor; let them go where they will, and wreck all the governments under heaven, they will be poor until they die.

Nothing is perhaps more notable in the average workman than his surprising idleness, and the candour with which he confesses to the failing. It has to me been always something of a relief to find the poor, as a general rule, so little oppressed with work. I can in consequence enjoy my own more fortunate beginning with a better grace. The other day I was living with a farmer in America, an old frontiersman, who had worked and fought, hunted and farmed, from his childhood up. He excused himself for his defective education on the ground that he had been overworked from first to last. Even now, he said, anxious as he was, he had never the time to take up a book. In consequence of this, I observed him closely; he was occupied for four or, at the extreme outside, for five hours out of the twenty-four, and then principally in walking; and the remainder of the day he passed in born idleness, either eating fruit or standing with his back against a door. I have known men do hard literary work all morning, and then undergo quite as much physical fatigue by way of relief as satisfied this powerful frontiersman for the day. He, at least, like all the educated class, did so much homage to industry as to persuade himself he was industrious. But the average mechanic recognises his idleness with effrontery; he has even, as I am told, organised it.

I give the story as it was told me, and it was told me for a fact. A man fell from a housetop in the city of Aberdeen, and was brought into hospital with broken bones. He was asked what was his trade, and replied that he was a *tapper*. No one had ever heard of such a thing before; the officials were filled with curiosity; they besought an explanation. It appeared that when a party of slaters were engaged upon a roof, they would now and then be taken with a fancy for the public-house. Now a seamstress, for example, might slip away from her work and no one be the wiser; but if these fellows adjourned, the tapping of the mallets would cease, and thus the neighbourhood be advertised of their defection. Hence the career of the tapper. He has to do the tapping and keep up an industrious bustle on the housetop during the absence of the slaters. When he taps for only one or two the thing is child's-play, but when he has to represent a whole troop, it is then that he earns his money in the sweat of his brow. Then must he bound from spot to spot, reduplicate, triplicate, sexduplicate his single personality, and swell and hasten his blows., until he produce a perfect illusion for the ear, and you would swear that a crowd of emulous masons were continuing merrily to roof the house. It must be a strange sight from an upper window.

I heard nothing on board of the tapper; but I was astonished at the stories told by my companions. Skulking, shirking, malingering, were all established tactics, it appeared. They could see no dishonesty where a man who is paid for an bones work gives half an hour's consistent idling in its place. Thus the tapper would refuse to watch for the police during a burglary, and call himself a honest man. It is not sufficiently recognised that our race detests to work. If I thought that I should have to work every day of my life as hard as I am working now, I should be tempted to give up the struggle. And the workman early begins on his career of toil. He has never had his fill of holidays in the past, and his prospect of holidays in the future is both distant and uncertain. In the circumstances, it would require a high degree of virtue not to snatch alleviations for the moment.

There were many good talkers on the ship; and I believe good talking of a certain sort is a common accomplishment among working men. Where books are comparatively scarce, a greater amount of information will be given and received by word of mouth; and this tends to produce good talkers, and, what is no less needful for conversation, good listeners. They could all tell a story with effect. I am sometimes tempted to think that the less literary class show always better in narration; they have so much more patience with detail, are so much less hurried to reach the points, and preserve so much juster a proportion among the facts. At the same time their talk is dry; they pursue a topic ploddingly, have not an agile fancy, do not throw sudden lights from unexpected quarters, and when the talk is over they often leave the matter where it was. They mark time instead of marching. They think only to argue, not to reach new conclusions, and use their reason rather as a weapon of offense than as a tool for self-improvement. Hence the talk of some of the cleverest was unprofitable in result, because there was no give and take; they would grant you as little as possible for premise, and begin to dispute under an oath to conquer or to die.

But the talk of a workman is apt to be more interesting than that of a wealthy merchant, because the thoughts, hopes, and fears of which the workman's life is built lie nearer to necessity and nature. They are more immediate to human life. An income calculated by the week is a far more human thing than one calculated by the year, and a small income, simply from its smallness, than a large one. I never wearied listening to the details of a workman's economy, because every item stood for some real pleasure. If he could afford pudding twice a week, you know that twice a week the man ate with genuine gusto and was physically happy; while if you learn that a rich man has seven courses a day, ten to one the half of them remain untasted, and the whole is but misspent money and a weariness to the flesh.

The difference between England and America to a working man was thus most humanly put to me by a fellow-passenger: 'In America,' said he, 'you get pies and puddings.' I do not hear enough, in economy books, of pies and pudding. A man lives in and for the delicacies, adornments, and accidental attributes of life, such as pudding to eat and pleasant books and theatres to occupy his leisure. The bare terms of existence would be rejected with contempt by all. If a man feeds on bread and butter, soup and porridge, his appetite grows wolfish after dainties. And the workman dwells in a borderland, and is always within sight of those cheerless regions where life is more difficult to sustain than worth sustaining. Every detail of our existence, where it is worth while to cross the ocean after pie and pudding, is made alive and enthralling by the presence of genuine desire; but it is all one to me whether Croesus has a hundred or a thousand thousands in the bank. There is more adventure in the life of the working man who descends as a common solder into the battle of life, than in that of the millionaire who sits apart in an office, like Von Moltke, and only directs the manoeuvres by telegraph. Give me to hear about the career of him who is in the thick of business; to whom one change of market means empty belly, and another a copious and savoury meal. This is not the philosophical, but the human side of economics; it interests like a story; and the life all who are thus situated partakes in a small way the charm of Robinson Crusoe; for every step is critical and human life is presented to you naked and verging to its lowest terms.

New York

As we drew near to New York I was at first amused, and then somewhat staggered, by the cautious and the grisly tales that went the round. You would have thought we were to land upon a cannibal island. You must speak to no one in the streets, as they would not leave you till you were rooked and beaten. You must enter a hotel with military precautions; for the least you had to apprehend was to awake next morning without money or baggage, or necessary raiment, a lone forked radish in a bed; and if the worst befell, you would instantly and mysteriously disappear from the ranks of mankind.

I have usually found such stories correspond to the least modicum of fact. Thus I was warned, I remember, against the roadside inns of the Cévennes, and that by a learned professor; and when I reached Pradelles the warning was explained—it was but the far-away rumour and reduplication of a single terrifying story already half a century old, and half forgotten in the theatre of the events. So I was tempted to make light of these reports against America. But we had on board with us a man whose evidence it would not do to put aside. He had come near these perils in the body; he had visited a robber inn. The public has an old and well-grounded favour for this class of incident, and shall be gratified to the best of my power.

My fellow-passenger, whom we shall call M'Naughten, had come from New York to Boston with a comrade, seeking work. They were a pair of rattling blades; and, leaving their baggage at the station, passed the day in beer saloons, and with congenial spirits, until midnight struck. Then they applied themselves to find a lodging, and walked the streets till two, knocking at houses of entertainment and being refused admittance, or themselves declining the terms. By two the inspiration of their liquor had begun to wear off; they were weary and humble, and after a great circuit found themselves in the same street where they had begun their search, and in front of a French hotel where they had already sought accommodation. Seeing the house still open, they returned to the charge. A man in a white cap sat in an office by the door. He seemed to welcome them more warmly than when they had first presented themselves, and the charge for the night had somewhat unaccountably fallen from a dollar to a quarter. They thought him ill-looking, but paid their quarter apiece, and were shown upstairs to the top of the house. There, in a small room, the man in the white cap wished them pleasant slumbers.

It was furnished with a bed, a chair, and some conveniences. The door did not lock on the inside; and the only sign of adornment was a couple of framed pictures, one close above the head of the bed, and the other opposite the foot, and both curtained, as we may sometimes see valuable water-colours, or the portraits of the dead, or works of art more than usually skittish in the subject. It was perhaps in the hope of finding something of this last description that M'Naughten's comrade pulled aside the curtain of the first. He was startlingly disappointed. There was no picture. The frame surrounded, and the curtain was designed to hide, an oblong aperture in the partition, through which they looked forth into the dark corridor. A person standing without could easily take a purse from under the pillow, or even strangle a sleeper as he lay abed. M'Naughten and his comrade stared at each other like Vasco's seamen, 'with a wild surmise'; and then the latter, catching up the lamp, ran to the other frame and roughly raised the curtain. There he stood, petrified; and M'Naughten, who had followed, grasped him by the wrist in terror. They could see into another room, larger in size than that which they occupied, where three men sat crouching and silent in the dark. For a second or so these five persons looked each other in the eyes, then the curtain was dropped, and M'Naughten and his friend made but one bolt of it out of the room and downstairs. The man in the white cap said nothing as they passed him; and they were so pleased to be once more in the open night that they gave up all notion of a bed, and walked the streets of Boston till the morning.

No one seemed much cast down by these stories, but all inquired after the address of a respectable hotel; and I, for my part, put myself under the conduct of Mr. Jones. Before noon of the second Sunday we sighted the low shores outside of New York harbour; the steerage passengers must remain on board to pass through Castle Garden on the following morning; but we of the second cabin made our escape along with the lords of the saloon; and by six o'clock Jones and I issued into West Street, sitting on some straw in the bottom of an open baggage-wagon. It rained miraculously; and from that moment till on the following night I left New York, there was scarce a lull, and no cessation of the downpour. The roadways were flooded; a loud strident noise of falling water filled the air; the restaurants smelt heavily of wet people and wet clothing.

It took us but a few minutes, though it cost us a good deal of money, to be rattled along West Street to our destination: 'Reunion House, No. 10 West Street, one minutes walk from Castle Garden; convenient to Castle Garden, the Steamboat Landings, California Steamers and Liverpool Ships; Board and Lodging per day 1 dollar, single meals 25 cents, lodging per night 25 cents; private rooms for families; no charge for storage or baggage; satisfaction guaranteed to all persons; Michael Mitchell, Proprietor.' Reunion House was, I may go the length of saying, a humble hostelry. You entered through a long bar-room, thence passed into a little dining-room, and thence into a still smaller kitchen. The furniture was of the plainest; but the bar was hung in the American taste, with encouraging and hospitable mottoes.

Jones was well known; we were received warmly; and two minutes afterwards I had refused a drink from the proprietor, and was going on, in my plain European fashion, to refuse a cigar, when Mr. Mitchell sternly interposed, and explained the situation. He was offering to treat me, it appeared, whenever an American bar-keeper proposes anything, it must be borne in mind that he is offering to treat; and if I did not want a drink, I must at least take the cigar. I took it bashfully, feeling I had begun my American career on the wrong foot. I did not enjoy that cigar; but this may have been from a variety of reasons, even the best cigar often failing to please if you smoke three-quarters of it in a drenching rain.

For many years America was to me a sort of promised land; 'westward the march of empire holds its way'; the race is for the moment to the young; what has been and what is we imperfectly and obscurely know; what is to be yet lies beyond the flight of our imaginations. Greece, Rome, and Judaea are gone by forever, leaving to generations the legacy of their accomplished work; China still endures, an old-inhabited house in the brand-new city of nations; England has already declined, since she has lost the States; and to these States, therefore, yet undeveloped, full of dark possibilities, and grown, like another Eve, from one rib out of the side of their own old land, the minds of young men in England turn naturally at a certain hopeful period of their age. It will be hard for an American to understand the spirit. But let him imagine a young man, who shall have grown up in an old and rigid circle, following bygone fashions and taught to distrust his own fresh instincts, and who now suddenly hears of a family of cousins, all about his own age, who keep house together by themselves and live far from restraint and tradition; let him imagine this, and he will have some imperfect notion of the sentiment with which spirited English youths turn to the thought of the American Republic. It seems to them as if, out west, the war of life was still conducted in the open air, and on free barbaric terms; as if it had not yet been narrowed into parlours, nor begun to be conducted, like some unjust and dreary arbitration, by compromise, costume forms of procedure, and sad, senseless self-denial. Which of these two he prefers, a man with any youth still left in him will decide rightly for himself. He would rather be houseless than denied a pass-key; rather go without food than partake of stalled ox in stiff, respectable society; rather be shot out of hand than direct his life according to the dictates of the world.

He knows or thinks nothing of the Maine Laws, the Puritan sourness, the fierce, sordid appetite for dollars, or the dreary existence of country towns. A few wild story-books which delighted his childhood form the imaginative basis of his picture of America. In course of time, there is added to this a great crowd of stimulating details—vast cities that grow up as by enchantment; the birds, that have gone south in autumn, returning with the spring to find thousands camped upon their marshes, and the lamps burning far and near along populous streets; forests that disappear like snow; countries larger than Britain that are cleared and settled, one man running forth with his household gods before another, while the bear and the Indian are yet scarce aware of their approach; oil that gushes from the earth; gold that is washed or quarried in the brooks or glens of the Sierras; and all that bustle, courage, action, and constant kaleidoscopic change that Walt Whitman has seized and set forth in his vigorous, cheerful, and loquacious verses.

Here I was at last in America, and was soon out upon New York streets, spying for things foreign. The place had to me an air of Liverpool; but such was the rain that not Paradise itself would have looked inviting. We were a party of four, under two umbrellas; Jones and I and two Scots lads, recent immigrants, and not indisposed to welcome a compatriot. They had been six weeks in New York, and neither of them had yet found a single job or earned a single halfpenny. Up to the present they were exactly out of pocket by the amount of the fare.

The lads soon left us. Now I had sworn by all my gods to have such a dinner as would rouse the dead; there was scarce any expense at which I should have hesitated; the devil was in it, but Jones and I should dine like heathen emperors. I set to work, asking after a restaurant; and I chose the wealthiest and most gastronomical-looking passers-by to ask from. Yet, although I had told them I was willing to pay anything in reason, one and all sent me off to cheap, fixed-price houses, where I would not have eaten that night for the cost of twenty dinners. I do not know if this were characteristic of New York, or whether it was only Jones and I who looked un-dinerly and discouraged enterprising suggestions. But at length, by our own sagacity, we found a French restaurant, where there was a French waiter, some fair French cooking, some so-called French wine, and French coffee to conclude the whole. I never entered into the feelings of Jack on land so completely as when I tasted that coffee.

I suppose we had one of the 'private rooms for families' at Reunion House. It was very small, furnished with a bed, a chair, and some clothes-pegs; and it derived all that was necessary for the life of the human animal through two borrowed lights; one looking into the passage, and the second opening, without sash, into another apartment, where three men fitfully snored, or in intervals of wakefulness, drearily mumbled to each other all night long. It will be observed that this was almost exactly the disposition of the room in M'Naughten's story. Jones had the bed; I pitched my camp upon the floor; he did not sleep until near morning, and I, for my part, never closed an eye.

At sunrise I heard a cannon fired; and shortly afterwards the men in the next room gave over snoring for good, and began to rustle over their toilettes. The sound of their voices as they talked was low and like that of people watching by the sick. Jones, who had at last begun to doze, tumbled and murmured, and every now and then opened unconscious eyes upon me where I lay. I found myself growing eerier and eerier, for I dare say I was a little fevered by my restless night, and hurried to dress and get downstairs.

You had to pass through the rain, which still fell thick and reso-nant, to reach a lavatory on the other side of the court. There were three basin-stands, and a few crumpled towels and pieces of wet soap, white and slippery like fish; nor should I forget a looking-glass and a pair of questionable combs. Another Scots lad was here, scrubbing his face with a good will. He had been three months in New York and had not yet found a single job nor earned a single halfpenny. Up to the present, he also was exactly out of pocket by the amount of the fare. I began to grow sick at heart for my fellow-emigrants.

Of my nightmare wanderings in New York I spare to tell. I had a thousand and one things to do; only the day to do them in, and a journey across the continent before me in the evening. It rained with patient fury; every now and then I had to get under cover for a while in order, so to speak, to give my mackintosh a rest; for under this continued drenching it began to grow damp on the inside. I went to banks, post-offices, railway-offices, restaurants, publishers, booksellers, money-changers, and wherever I went a pool would gather about my feet, and those who were careful of their floors would look on with an unfriendly eye. Wherever I went, too, the same traits struck me: the people were all surprisingly rude and surprisingly kind. The money-changer cross-questioned me like a French commissary, asking my age, my business, my average income, and my destination, beating down my attempts at evasion, and receiving my answers in silence; and yet when all was over, he shook hands with me up to the elbows, and sent his lad nearly a quarter of a mile in the rain to get me books at a reduction. Again, in a very large publishing and bookselling establishment, a man, who seemed to be the manager, received me as I had certainly never before been received in any human shop, indicated squarely that he put no faith in my honesty, and refused to look up the names of books or give me the slightest help or information, on the ground, like the steward, that it was none of his business. I lost my temper at last, said I was a stranger in America and not learned in their etiquette; but I would assure him, if he went to any bookseller in England, of more handsome usage. The boast was perhaps exaggerated; but like many a long shot, it struck the gold. The manager passed at once from one extreme to the other; I may say that from that moment he loaded me with kindness; he gave me all sorts of good advice, wrote me down addresses, and came bareheaded into the rain to point me out a restaurant, where I might lunch, nor even then did he seem to think that he had done enough. These are (it is as well to be bold in statement) the manners of America. It is this same opposition that has most struck me in people of almost all classes and from east to west. By the time a man had about strung me up to be the death of him by his insulting behaviour, he himself would be just upon the point of melting into confidence and serviceable attentions. Yet I suspect, although I have met with the like in so many parts, that this must be the character of some particular state or group of states, for in America, and this again in all classes, you will find some of the softest-mannered gentlemen in the world.

I was so wet when I got back to Mitchell's toward the evening, that I had simply to divest myself of my shoes, socks, and trousers, and leave them behind for the benefit of New York city. No fire could have dried them ere I had to start; and to pack them in their present condition was to spread ruin among my other possessions. With a heavy heart I said farewell to them as they lay a pulp in the middle of a pool upon the floor of Mitchell's kitchen. I wonder if they are dry by now. Mitchell hired a man to carry my baggage to the station, which was hard by, accompanied me thither himself, and recommended me to the particular attention of the officials. No one could have been kinder. Those who are out of pocket may go safely to Reunion House, where they will get decent meals and find an honest and obliging landlord. I owed him this word of thanks, before I enter fairly on the second[1] and far less agreeable chapter of my emigrant experience.

---

[1]   The Second Part here referred to is entitled 'ACROSS THE PLAINS,' and is printed in the volume so entitled, together with other Memories and Essays.

CHAPTER II—COCKERMOUTH AND KESWICK—A FRAGMENT—1871

Very much as a painter half closes his eyes so that some salient unity may disengage itself from among the crowd of details, and what he sees may thus form itself into a whole; very much on the same principle, I may say, I allow a considerable lapse of time to intervene between any of my little journeyings and the attempt to chronicle them. I cannot describe a thing that is before me at the moment, or that has been before me only a very little while before; I must allow my recollections to get thoroughly strained free from all chaff till nothing be except the pure gold; allow my memory to choose out what is truly memorable by a process of natural selection; and I piously believe that in this way I ensure the Survival of the Fittest. If I make notes for future use, or if I am obliged to write letters during the course of my little excursion, I so interfere with the process that I can never again find out what is worthy of being preserved, or what should be given in full length, what in torso, or what merely in profile. This process of incubation may be unreasonably prolonged; and I am somewhat afraid that I have made this mistake with the present journey. Like a bad daguerreotype, great part of it has been entirely lost; I can tell you nothing about the beginning and nothing about the end; but the doings of some fifty or sixty hours about the middle remain quite distinct and definite, like a little patch of sunshine on a long, shadowy plain, or the one spot on an old picture that has been restored by the dexterous hand of the cleaner. I remember a tale of an old Scots minister called upon suddenly to preach, who had hastily snatched an old sermon out of his study and found himself in the pulpit before he noticed that the rats had been making free with his manuscript and eaten the first two or three pages away; he gravely explained to the congregation how he found himself situated: 'And now,' said he, 'let us just begin where the rats have left off.' I must follow the divine's example, and take up the thread of my discourse where it first distinctly issues from the limbo of forgetfulness.

Cockermouth

I was lighting my pipe as I stepped out of the inn at Cockermouth, and did not raise my head until I was fairly in the street. When I did so, it flashed upon me that I was in England; the evening sunlight lit up English houses, English faces, an English conformation of street,—as it were, an English atmosphere blew against my face. There is nothing perhaps more puzzling (if one thing in sociology can ever really be more unaccountable than another) than the great gulf that is set between England and Scotland—a gulf so easy in appearance, in reality so difficult to traverse. Here are two people almost identical in blood; pent up together on one small island, so that their intercourse (one would have thought) must be as close as that of prisoners who shared one cell of the Bastille; the same in language and religion; and yet a few years of quarrelsome isolation—a mere forenoon's tiff, as one may call it, in comparison with the great historical cycles—has so separated their thoughts and ways that not unions, not mutual dangers, nor steamers, nor railways, nor all the king's horses and all the king's men, seem able to obliterate the broad distinction. In the trituration of another century or so the corners may disappear; but in the meantime, in the year of grace 1871, I was as much in a new country as if I had been walking out of the Hotel St. Antoine at Antwerp.

I felt a little thrill of pleasure at my heart as I realised the change, and strolled away up the street with my hands behind my back, noting in a dull, sensual way how foreign, and yet how friendly, were the slopes of the gables and the colour of the tiles, and even the demeanour and voices of the gossips round about me.

Wandering in this aimless humour, I turned up a lane and found myself following the course of the bright little river. I passed first one and then another, then a third, several couples out love-making in the spring evening; and a consequent feeling of loneliness was beginning to grow upon me, when I came to a dam across the river, and a mill—a great, gaunt promontory of building,—half on dry ground and half arched over the stream. The road here drew in its shoulders and crept through between the landward extremity of the mill and a little garden enclosure, with a small house and a large signboard within its privet hedge. I was pleased to fancy this an inn, and drew little etchings in fancy of a sanded parlour, and three-cornered spittoons, and a society of parochial gossips seated within over their churchwardens; but as I drew near, the board displayed its superscription, and I could read the name of Smethurst, and the designation of 'Canadian Felt Hat Manufacturers.' There was no more hope of evening fellowship, and I could only stroll on by the river-side, under the trees. The water was dappled with slanting sunshine, and dusted all over with a little mist of flying insects. There were some amorous ducks, also, whose lovemaking reminded me of what I had seen a little farther down. But the road grew sad, and I grew weary; and as I was perpetually haunted with the terror of a return of the tie that had been playing such ruin in my head a week ago, I turned and went back to the inn, and supper, and my bed.

The next morning, at breakfast, I communicated to the smart waitress my intention of continuing down the coast and through Whitehaven to Furness, and, as I might have expected, I was instantly confronted by that last and most worrying form of interference, that chooses to introduce tradition and authority into the choice of a man's own pleasures. I can excuse a person combating my religious or philosophical heresies, because them I have deliberately accepted, and am ready to justify by present argument. But I do not seek to justify my pleasures. If I prefer tame scenery to grand, a little hot sunshine over lowland parks and woodlands to the war of the elements round the summit of Mont Blanc; or if I prefer a pipe of mild tobacco, and the company of one or two chosen companions, to a ball where I feel myself very hot, awkward, and weary, I merely state these preferences as facts, and do not seek to establish them as principles. This is not the general rule, however, and accordingly the waitress was shocked, as one might be at a heresy, to hear the route that I had sketched out for myself. Everybody who came to Cockermouth for pleasure, it appeared, went on to Keswick. It was in vain that I put up a little plea for the liberty of the subject; it was in vain that I said I should prefer to go to Whitehaven. I was told that there was 'nothing to see there'—that weary, hackneyed, old falsehood; and at last, as the handmaiden began to look really concerned, I gave way, as men always do in such circumstances, and agreed that I was to leave for Keswick by a train in the early evening.

An Evangelist

Cockermouth itself, on the same authority, was a Place with 'nothing to see'; nevertheless I saw a good deal, and retain a pleasant, vague picture of the town and all its surroundings. I might have dodged happily enough all day about the main street and up to the castle and in and out of byways, but the curious attraction that leads a person in a strange place to follow, day after day, the same round, and to make set habits for himself in a week or ten days, led me half unconsciously up the same, road that I had gone the evening before. When I came up to the hat manufactory, Smethurst himself was standing in the garden gate. He was brushing one Canadian felt hat, and several others had been put to await their turn one above the other on his own head, so that he looked something like the typical Jew old-clothes man. As I drew near, he came sidling out of the doorway to accost me, with so curious an expression on his face that I instinctively prepared myself to apologise for some unwitting trespass. His first question rather confirmed me in this belief, for it was whether or not he had seen me going up this way last night; and after having answered in the affirmative, I waited in some alarm for the rest of my indictment. But the good man's heart was full of peace; and he stood there brushing his hats and prattling on about fishing, and walking, and the pleasures of convalescence, in a bright shallow stream that kept me pleased and interested, I could scarcely say how. As he went on, he warmed to his subject, and laid his hats aside to go along the water-side and show me where the large trout commonly lay, underneath an overhanging bank; and he was much disappointed, for my sake, that there were none visible just then. Then he wandered off on to another tack, and stood a great while out in the middle of a meadow in the hot sunshine, trying to make out that he had known me before, or, if not me, some friend of mine, merely, I believe, out of a desire that we should feel more friendly and at our ease with one another. At last he made a little speech to me, of which I wish I could recollect the very words, for they were so simple and unaffected that they put all the best writing and speaking to the blush; as it is, I can recall only the sense, and that perhaps imperfectly. He began by saying that he had little things in his past life that it gave him especial pleasure to recall; and that the faculty of receiving such sharp impressions had now died out in himself, but must at my age be still quite lively and active. Then he told me that he had a little raft afloat on the river above the dam which he was going to lend me, in order that I might be able to look back, in after years, upon having done so, and get great pleasure from the recollection. Now, I have a friend of my own who will forgo present enjoyments and suffer much present inconvenience for the sake of manufacturing 'a reminiscence' for himself; but there was something singularly refined in this pleasure that the hatmaker found in making reminiscences for others; surely no more simple or unselfish luxury can be imagined. After he had unmoored his little embarkation, and seen me safely shoved off into midstream, he ran away back to his hats with the air of a man who had only just recollected that he had anything to do.

I did not stay very long on the raft. It ought to have been very nice punting about there in the cool shade of the trees, or sitting moored to an over-hanging root; but perhaps the very notion that I was bound in gratitude specially to enjoy my little cruise, and cherish its recollection, turned the whole thing from a pleasure into a duty. Be that as it may, there is no doubt that I soon wearied and came ashore again, and that it gives me more pleasure to recall the man himself and his simple, happy conversation, so full of gusto and sympathy, than anything possibly connected with his crank, insecure embarkation. In order to avoid seeing him, for I was not a little ashamed of myself for having failed to enjoy his treat sufficiently, I determined to continue up the river, and, at all prices, to find some other way back into the town in time for dinner. As I went, I was thinking of Smethurst with admiration; a look into that man's mind was like a retrospect over the smiling champaign of his past life, and very different from the Sinai-gorges up which one looks for a terrified moment into the dark souls of many good, many wise, and many prudent men. I cannot be very grateful to such men for their excellence, and wisdom, and prudence. I find myself facing as stoutly as I can a hard, combative existence, full of doubt, difficulties, defeats, disappointments, and dangers, quite a hard enough life without their dark countenances at my elbow, so that what I want is a happy-minded Smethurst placed here and there at ugly corners of my life's wayside, preaching his gospel of quiet and contentment.

Another

I was shortly to meet with an evangelist of another stamp. After I had forced my way through a gentleman's grounds, I came out on the high road, and sat down to rest myself on a heap of stones at the top of a long hill, with Cockermouth lying snugly at the bottom. An Irish beggar-woman, with a beautiful little girl by her side, came up to ask for alms, and gradually fell to telling me the little tragedy of her life. Her own sister, she told me, had seduced her husband from her after many years of married life, and the pair had fled, leaving her destitute, with the little girl upon her hands. She seemed quite hopeful and cheery, and, though she was unaffectedly sorry for the loss of her husband's earnings, she made no pretence of despair at the loss of his affection; some day she would meet the fugitives, and the law would see her duly righted, and in the meantime the smallest contribution was gratefully received. While she was telling all this in the most matter-of-fact way, I had been noticing the approach of a tall man, with a high white hat and darkish clothes. He came up the hill at a rapid pace, and joined our little group with a sort of half-salutation. Turning at once to the woman, he asked her in a business-like way whether she had anything to do, whether she were a Catholic or a Protestant, whether she could read, and so forth; and then, after a few kind words and some sweeties to the child, he despatched the mother with some tracts about Biddy and the Priest, and the Orangeman's Bible. I was a little amused at his abrupt manner, for he was still a young man, and had somewhat the air of a navy officer; but he tackled me with great solemnity. I could make fun of what he said, for I do not think it was very wise; but the subject does not appear to me just now in a jesting light, so I shall only say that he related to me his own conversion, which had been effected (as is very often the case) through the agency of a gig accident, and that, after having examined me and diagnosed my case, he selected some suitable tracts from his repertory, gave them to me, and, bidding me God-speed, went on his way.

Last of Smethurst

That evening I got into a third-class carriage on my way for Keswick, and was followed almost immediately by a burly man in brown clothes. This fellow-passenger was seemingly ill at ease, and kept continually putting his head out of the window, and asking the bystanders if they saw *him* coming. At last, when the train was already in motion, there was a commotion on the platform, and a way was left clear to our carriage door. *He* had arrived. In the hurry I could just see Smethurst, red and panting, thrust a couple of clay pipes into my companion's outstretched band, and hear him crying his farewells after us as we slipped out of the station at an ever accelerating pace. I said something about it being a close run, and the broad man, already engaged in filling one of the pipes, assented, and went on to tell me of his own stupidity in forgetting a necessary, and of how his friend had good-naturedly gone down town at the last moment to supply the omission. I mentioned that I had seen Mr. Smethurst already, and that he had been very polite to me; and we fell into a discussion of the hatter's merits that lasted some time and left us quite good friends at its conclusion. The topic was productive of good-will. We exchanged tobacco and talked about the season, and agreed at last that we should go to the same hotel at Keswick and sup in company. As he had some business in the town which would occupy him some hour or so, on our arrival I was to improve the time and go down to the lake, that I might see a glimpse of the promised wonders.

The night had fallen already when I reached the water-side, at a place where many pleasure-boats are moored and ready for hire; and as I went along a stony path, between wood and water, a strong wind blew in gusts from the far end of the lake. The sky was covered with flying scud; and, as this was ragged, there was quite a wild chase of shadow and moon-glimpse over the surface of the shuddering water. I had to hold my hat on, and was growing rather tired, and inclined to go back in disgust, when a little incident occurred to break the tedium. A sudden and violent squall of wind sundered the low underwood, and at the same time there came one of those brief discharges of moonlight, which leaped into the opening thus made, and showed me three girls in the prettiest flutter and disorder. It was as though they had sprung out of the ground. I accosted them very politely in my capacity of stranger, and requested to be told the names of all manner of hills and woods and places that I did not wish to know, and we stood together for a while and had an amusing little talk. The wind, too, made himself of the party, brought the colour into their faces, and gave them enough to do to repress their drapery; and one of them, amid much giggling, had to pirouette round and round upon her toes (as girls do) when some specially strong gust had got the advantage over her. They were just high enough up in the social order not to be afraid to speak to a gentleman; and just low enough to feel a little tremor, a nervous consciousness of wrong-doing—of stolen waters, that gave a considerable zest to our most innocent interview. They were as much discomposed and fluttered, indeed, as if I had been a wicked baron proposing to elope with the whole trio; but they showed no inclination to go away, and I had managed to get them off hills and waterfalls and on to more promising subjects, when a young man was descried coming along the path from the direction of Keswick. Now whether he was the young man of one of my friends, or the brother of one of them, or indeed the brother of all, I do not know; but they incontinently said that they must be going, and went away up the path with friendly salutations. I need not say that I found the lake and the moonlight rather dull after their departure, and speedily found my way back to potted herrings and whisky-and-water in the commercial room with my late fellow-traveller. In the smoking-room there was a tall dark man with a moustache, in an ulster coat, who had got the best place and was monopolising most of the talk; and, as I came in, a whisper came round to me from both sides, that this was the manager of a London theatre. The presence of such a man was a great event for Keswick, and I must own that the manager showed himself equal to his position. He had a large fat pocket-book, from which he produced poem after poem, written on the backs of letters or hotel-bills; and nothing could be more humorous than his recitation of these elegant extracts, except perhaps the anecdotes with which he varied the entertainment. Seeing, I suppose, something less countrified in my appearance than in most of the company, he singled me out to corroborate some statements as to the depravity and vice of the aristocracy, and when he went on to describe some gilded saloon experiences, I am proud to say that he honoured my sagacity with one little covert wink before a second time appealing to me for confirmation. The wink was not thrown away; I went in up to the elbows with the manager, until I think that some of the glory of that great man settled by reflection upon me, and that I was as noticeably the second person in the smoking-room as he was the first. For a young man, this was a position of some distinction, I think you will admit. . . .

CHAPTER III—AN AUTUMN EFFECT—1875

'Nous ne décrivons jamais mieux la nature que lorsque nous nous efforçons d'exprimer sobrement et simplement l'impression que nous en avons reçue.'—M. ANDRÉ THEURIET, *'L'Automne dans les Bois,'* Revue des Deux Mondes, 1st Oct. 1874, p.562.[2]

A country rapidly passed through under favourable auspices may leave upon us a unity of impression that would only be disturbed and dissipated if we stayed longer. Clear vision goes with the quick foot. Things fall for us into a sort of natural perspective when we see them for a moment in going by; we generalise boldly and simply, and are gone before the sun is overcast, before the rain falls, before the season can steal like a dial-hand from his figure, before the lights and shadows, shifting round towards nightfall, can show us the other side of things, and belie what they showed us in the morning. We expose our mind to the landscape (as we would expose the prepared plate in the camera) for the moment only during which the effect endures; and we are away before the effect can change. Hence we shall have in our memories a long scroll of continuous wayside pictures, all imbued already with the prevailing sentiment of the season, the weather and the landscape, and certain to be unified more and more, as time goes on, by the unconscious processes of thought. So that we who have only looked at a country over our shoulder, so to speak, as we went by, will have a conception of it far more memorable and articulate than a man who has lived there all his

---

2   I had nearly finished the transcription of the following pages when I saw on a friend's table the number containing the piece from which this sentence is extracted, and, struck with a similarity of title, took it home with me and read it with indescribable satisfaction. I do not know whether I more envy M. Theuriet the pleasure of having written this delightful article, or the reader the pleasure, which I hope he has still before him, of reading it once and again, and lingering over the passages that please him most.

life from a child upwards, and had his impression of to-day modified by that of to-morrow, and belied by that of the day after, till at length the stable characteristics of the country are all blotted out from him behind the confusion of variable effect.

I begin my little pilgrimage in the most enviable of all humours: that in which a person, with a sufficiency of money and a knapsack, turns his back on a town and walks forward into a country of which he knows only by the vague report of others. Such an one has not surrendered his will and contracted for the next hundred miles, like a man on a railway. He may change his mind at every finger-post, and, where ways meet, follow vague preferences freely and go the low road or the high, choose the shadow or the sun-shine, suffer himself to be tempted by the lane that turns immediately into the woods, or the broad road that lies open before him into the distance, and shows him the far-off spires of some city, or a range of mountain-tops, or a rim of sea, perhaps, along a low horizon. In short, he may gratify his every whim and fancy, without a pang of reproving conscience, or the least jostle to his self-respect. It is true, however, that most men do not possess the faculty of free action, the priceless gift of being able to live for the moment only; and as they begin to go forward on their journey, they will find that they have made for themselves new fetters. Slight projects they may have entertained for a moment, half in jest, become iron laws to them, they know not why. They will be led by the nose by these vague reports of which I spoke above; and the mere fact that their informant mentioned one village and not another will compel their footsteps with inexplicable power. And yet a little while, yet a few days of this fictitious liberty, and they will begin to hear imperious voices calling on them to return; and some passion, some duty, some worthy or unworthy expectation, will set its hand upon their shoulder and lead them back into the old paths. Once and again we have all made the experiment. We know the end of it right well. And yet if we make it for the hundredth time to-morrow: it will have the same charm as ever; our heart will beat and our eyes will be bright, as we leave the town behind us, and we shall feel once again (as we have felt so often before) that we are cutting ourselves loose for ever from our whole past life, with all its sins and follies and circumscriptions, and go forward as a new creature into a new world.

It was well, perhaps, that I had this first enthusiasm to encourage me up the long hill above High Wycombe; for the day was a bad day for walking at best, and now began to draw towards afternoon, dull, heavy, and lifeless. A pall of grey cloud covered the sky, and its colour reacted on the colour of the landscape. Near at hand, indeed, the hedgerow trees were still fairly green, shot through with bright autumnal yellows, bright as sunshine. But a little way off, the solid bricks of woodland that lay squarely on slope and hill-top were not green, but russet and grey, and ever less russet and more grey as they drew off into the distance. As they drew off into the distance, also, the woods seemed to mass themselves together, and lie thin and straight, like clouds, upon the limit of one's view. Not that this massing was complete, or gave the idea of any extent of forest, for every here and there the trees would break up and go down into a valley in open order, or stand in long Indian file along the horizon, tree after tree relieved, foolishly enough, against the sky. I say foolishly enough, although I have seen the effect employed cleverly in art, and such long line of single trees thrown out against the customary sunset of a Japanese picture with a certain fantastic effect that was not to be despised; but this was over water and level land, where it did not jar, as here, with the soft contour of hills and valleys. The whole scene had an indefinable look of being painted, the colour was so abstract and correct, and there was something so sketchy and merely impressional about these distant single trees on the horizon that one was forced to think of it all as of a clever French landscape. For it is rather in nature that we see resemblance to art, than in art to nature; and we say a hundred times, 'How like a picture!' for once that we say, 'How like the truth!' The forms in which we learn to think of landscape are forms that we have got from painted canvas. Any man can see and understand a picture; it is reserved for the few to separate anything out of the confusion of nature, and see that distinctly and with intelligence.

The sun came out before I had been long on my way; and as I had got by that time to the top of the ascent, and was now treading a labyrinth of confined by-roads, my whole view brightened considerably in colour, for it was the distance only that was grey and cold, and the distance I could see no longer. Overhead there was a wonderful carolling of larks which seemed to follow me as I went. Indeed, during all the time I was in that country the larks did not desert me. The air was alive with them from High Wycombe to Tring; and as, day after day, their 'shrill delight' fell upon me out of the vacant sky, they began to take such a prominence over other conditions, and form so integral a part of my conception of the country, that I could have baptized it 'The Country of Larks.' This, of course, might just as well have been in early spring; but everything else was deeply imbued with the sentiment of the later year. There was no stir of insects in the grass. The sunshine was more golden, and gave less heat than summer sunshine; and the shadows under the hedge were somewhat blue and misty. It was only in autumn that you could have seen the mingled green and yellow of the elm foliage, and the fallen leaves that lay about the road, and covered the surface of wayside pools so thickly that the sun was reflected only here and there from little joints and pinholes in that brown coat of proof; or that your ear would have been troubled, as you went forward, by the occasional report of fowling-pieces from all directions and all degrees of distance.

For a long time this dropping fire was the one sign of human activity that came to disturb me as I walked. The lanes were profoundly still. They would have been sad but for the sunshine and the singing of the larks. And as it was, there came over me at times a feeling of isolation that was not disagreeable, and yet was enough to make me quicken my steps eagerly when I saw some one before me on the road. This fellow-voyager proved to be no less a person than the parish constable. It had occurred to me that in a district which was so little populous and so well wooded, a criminal of any intelligence might play hide-and-seek with the authorities for months; and this idea was strengthened by the aspect of the portly constable as he walked by my side with deliberate dignity and turned-out toes. But a few minutes' converse set my heart at rest. These rural criminals are very tame birds, it appeared. If my informant did not immediately lay his hand on an offender, he was content to wait; some evening after nightfall there would come a tap at his door, and the outlaw, weary of outlawry, would give himself quietly up to undergo sentence, and resume his position in the life of the country-side. Married men caused him no disquietude whatever; he had them fast by the foot. Sooner or later they would come back to see their wives, a peeping neighbour would pass the word, and my portly constable would walk quietly over and take the bird sitting. And if there were a few who had no particular ties in the neighbourhood, and preferred to shift into another county when they fell into trouble, their departure moved the placid constable in no degree. He was of Dogberry's opinion; and if a man would not stand in the Prince's name, he took no note of him, but let him go, and thanked God he was rid of a knave. And surely the crime and the law were in admirable keeping; rustic constable was well met with rustic offender. The officer sitting at home over a bit of fire until the criminal came to visit him, and the criminal coming—it was a fair match. One felt as if this must have been the order in that delightful seaboard Bohemia where Florizel and Perdita courted in such sweet accents, and the Puritan sang Psalms to hornpipes, and the four-and-twenty shearers danced with nosegays in their bosoms, and chanted their three songs apiece at the old shepherd's festival; and one could not help picturing to oneself what havoc among good peoples purses, and tribulation for benignant constables, might be worked here by the arrival, over stile and footpath, of a new Autolycus.

Bidding good-morning to my fellow-traveller, I left the road and struck across country. It was rather a revelation to pass from between the hedgerows and find quite a bustle on the other side, a great coming and going of school-children upon by-paths, and, in every second field, lusty horses and stout country-folk a-ploughing. The way I followed took me through many fields thus occupied, and through many strips of plantation, and then over a little space of smooth turf, very pleasant to the feet, set with tall fir-trees and clamorous with rooks making ready for the winter, and so back again into the quiet road. I was now not far from the end of my day's journey. A few hundred yards farther, and, passing through a gap in the hedge, I began to go down hill through a pretty extensive tract of young beeches. I was soon in shadow myself, but the afternoon sun still coloured the upmost boughs of the wood, and made a fire over my head in the autumnal foliage. A little faint vapour lay among the slim tree-stems in the bottom of the hollow; and from farther up I heard from time to time an outburst of gross laughter, as though clowns were making merry in the bush. There was something about the atmosphere that brought all sights and sounds home to one with a singular purity, so that I felt as if my senses had been washed with water. After I had crossed the little zone of mist, the path began to remount the hill; and just as I, mounting along with it, had got back again, from the head downwards, into the thin golden sunshine, I saw in front of me a donkey tied to a tree. Now, I have a certain liking for donkeys, principally, I believe, because of the delightful things that Sterne has written of them. But this was not after the pattern of the ass at Lyons. He was of a white colour, that seemed to fit him rather for rare festal occasions than for constant drudgery. Besides, he was very small, and of the daintiest portions you can imagine in a donkey. And so, sure enough, you had only to look at him to see he had never worked. There was something too roguish and wanton in his face, a look too like that of a schoolboy or a street Arab, to have survived much cudgelling. It was plain that these feet had kicked off sportive children oftener than they had plodded with a freight through miry lanes. He was altogether a fine-weather, holiday sort of donkey; and though he was just then somewhat solemnised and rueful, he still gave proof of the levity of his disposition by impudently wagging his ears at me as I drew near. I say he was somewhat solemnised just then; for, with the admirable instinct of all men and animals under restraint, he had so wound and wound the halter about the tree that he could go neither back nor forwards, nor so much as put down his head to browse. There he stood, poor rogue, part puzzled, part angry, part, I believe, amused. He had not given up hope, and dully revolved the problem in his head, giving ever and again another jerk at the few inches of free rope that still remained unwound. A humorous sort of sympathy for the creature took hold upon me. I went up, and, not without some trouble on my part, and much distrust and resistance on the part of Neddy, got him forced backwards until the whole length of the halter was set loose, and he was once more as free a donkey as I dared to make him. I was pleased (as people are) with this friendly action to a fellow-creature in tribulation, and glanced back over my shoulder to see how he was profiting by his freedom. The brute was looking after me; and no sooner did he catch my eye than he put up his long white face into the air, pulled an impudent mouth at me, and began to bray derisively. If ever any one person made a grimace at another, that donkey made a grimace at me. The hardened ingratitude of his behaviour, and the impertinence that inspired his whole face as he curled up his lip, and showed his teeth, and began to bray, so tickled me, and was so much in keeping with what I had imagined to myself about his character, that I could not find it in my heart to be angry, and burst into a peal of hearty laughter. This seemed to strike the ass as a repartee, so he brayed at me again by way of rejoinder; and we went on for a while, braying and laughing, until I began to grow aweary of it, and, shouting a derisive farewell, turned to pursue my way. In so doing—it was like going suddenly into cold water—I found myself face to face with a prim little old maid. She was all in a flutter, the poor old dear! She had concluded beyond question that this must be a lunatic who stood laughing aloud at a white donkey in the placid beech-woods. I was sure, by her face, that she had already recommended her spirit most religiously to Heaven, and prepared herself for the worst. And so, to reassure her, I uncovered and besought her, after a very staid fashion, to put me on my way to Great Missenden. Her voice trembled a little, to be sure, but I think her mind was set at rest; and she told me, very explicitly, to follow the path until I came to the end of the wood, and then I should see the village below me in the bottom of the valley. And, with mutual courtesies, the little old maid and I went on our respective ways.

Nor had she misled me. Great Missenden was close at hand, as she had said, in the trough of a gentle valley, with many great elms about it. The smoke from its chimneys went up pleasantly in the afternoon sunshine. The sleepy hum of a threshing-machine filled the neighbouring fields and hung about the quaint street corners. A little above, the church sits well back on its haunches against the hillside—an attitude for a church, you know, that makes it look as if it could be ever so much higher if it liked; and the trees grew about it thickly, so as to make a density of shade in the churchyard. A very quiet place it looks; and yet I saw many boards and posters about threatening dire punishment against those who broke the church windows or defaced the precinct, and offering rewards for the apprehension of those who had done the like already. It was fair day in Great Missenden. There were three stalls set up, sub jove, for the sale of pastry and cheap toys; and a great number of holiday children thronged about the stalls and noisily invaded every corner of the straggling village. They came round me by coveys, blowing simultaneously upon penny trumpets as though they imagined I should fall to pieces like the battlements of Jericho. I noticed one among them who could make a wheel of himself like a London boy, and seemingly enjoyed a grave pre-eminence upon the strength of the accomplishment. By and by, however, the trumpets began to weary me, and I went indoors, leaving the fair, I fancy, at its height.

Night had fallen before I ventured forth again. It was pitch-dark in the village street, and the darkness seemed only the greater for a light here and there in an uncurtained window or from an open door. Into one such window I was rude enough to peep, and saw within a charming genre picture. In a room, all white wainscot and crimson wall-paper, a perfect gem of colour after the black, empty darkness in which I had been groping, a pretty girl was telling a story, as well as I could make out, to an attentive child upon her knee, while an old woman sat placidly dozing over the fire. You may be sure I was not behindhand with a story for myself—a good old story after the manner of G. P. R. James and the village melodramas, with a wicked squire, and poachers, and an attorney, and a virtuous young man with a genius for mechanics, who should love, and protect, and ultimately marry the girl in the crimson room. Baudelaire has a few dainty sentences on the fancies that we are inspired with when we look through a window into other people's lives; and I think Dickens has somewhere enlarged on the same text. The subject, at least, is one that I am seldom weary of entertaining. I remember, night after night, at Brussels, watching a good family sup together, make merry, and retire to rest; and night after night I waited to see the candles lit, and the salad made, and the last salutations dutifully exchanged, without any abatement of interest. Night after night I found the scene rivet my attention and keep me awake in bed with all manner of quaint imaginations. Much of the pleasure of the Arabian Nights hinges upon this Asmodean interest; and we are not weary of lifting other people's roofs, and going about behind the scenes of life with the Caliph and the serviceable Giaffar. It is a salutary exercise, besides; it is salutary to get out of ourselves and see people living together in perfect unconsciousness of our existence, as they will live when we are gone. If to-morrow the blow falls, and the worst of our ill fears is realised, the girl will none the less tell stories to the child on her lap in the cottage at Great Missenden, nor the good Belgians light their candle, and mix their salad, and go orderly to bed.

The next morning was sunny overhead and damp underfoot, with a thrill in the air like a reminiscence of frost. I went up into the sloping garden behind the inn and smoked a pipe pleasantly enough, to the tune of my landlady's lamentations over sundry cabbages and cauliflowers that had been spoiled by caterpillars. She had been so much pleased in the summer-time, she said, to see the garden all hovered over by white butterflies. And now, look at the end of it! She could nowise reconcile this with her moral sense. And, indeed, unless these butterflies are created with a side-look to the composition of improving apologues, it is not altogether easy, even for people who have read Hegel and Dr. M'Cosh, to decide intelligibly upon the issue raised. Then I fell into a long and abstruse calculation with my landlord; having for object to compare the distance driven by him during eight years' service on the box of the Wendover coach with the girth of the round world itself. We tackled the question most conscientiously, made all necessary allowance for Sundays and leap-years, and were just coming to a triumphant conclusion of our labours when we were stayed by a small lacuna in my information. I did not know the circumference of the earth. The landlord knew it, to be sure—plainly he had made the same calculation twice and once before,—but he wanted confidence in his own figures, and from the moment I showed myself so poor a second seemed to lose all interest in the result.

Wendover (which was my next stage) lies in the same valley with Great Missenden, but at the foot of it, where the hills trend off on either hand like a coast-line, and a great hemisphere of plain lies, like a sea, before one, I went up a chalky road, until I had a good outlook over the place. The vale, as it opened out into the plain, was shallow, and a little bare, perhaps, but full of graceful convolutions. From the level to which I have now attained the fields were exposed before me like a map, and I could see all that bustle of autumn field-work which had been hid from me yesterday behind the hedgerows, or shown to me only for a moment as I followed the footpath. Wendover lay well down in the midst, with mountains of foliage about it. The great plain stretched away to the northward, variegated near at hand with the quaint pattern of the fields, but growing ever more and more indistinct, until it became a mere hurly-burly of trees and bright crescents of river, and snatches of slanting road, and finally melted into the ambiguous cloud-land over the horizon. The sky was an opal-grey, touched here and there with blue, and with certain faint russets that looked as if they were reflections of the colour of the autumnal woods below. I could hear the ploughmen shouting to their horses, the uninterrupted carol of larks innumerable overhead, and, from a field where the shepherd was marshalling his flock, a sweet tumultuous tinkle of sheep-bells. All these noises came to me very thin and distinct in the clear air. There was a wonderful sentiment of distance and atmosphere about the day and the place.

I mounted the hill yet farther by a rough staircase of chalky foot-holds cut in the turf. The hills about Wendover and, as far as I could see, all the hills in Buckinghamshire, wear a sort of hood of beech plantation; but in this particular case the hood had been suffered to extend itself into something more like a cloak, and hung down about the shoulders of the hill in wide folds, instead of lying flatly along the summit. The trees grew so close, and their boughs were so matted to-gether, that the whole wood looked as dense as a bush of heather. The prevailing colour was a dull, smouldering red, touched here and there with vivid yellow. But the autumn had scarce advanced beyond the out-works; it was still almost summer in the heart of the wood; and as soon as I had scrambled through the hedge, I found myself in a dim green forest atmosphere under eaves of virgin foliage. In places where the wood had itself for a background and the trees were massed together thickly, the colour became intensified and almost gem-like: a perfect fire green, that seemed none the less green for a few specks of autumn gold. None of the trees were of any considerable age or stature; but they grew well together, I have said; and as the road turned and wound among them, they fell into pleasant groupings and broke the light up pleasantly. Sometimes there would be a colonnade of slim, straight tree-stems with the light running down them as down the shafts of pillars, that looked as if it ought to lead to something, and led only to a corner of sombre and intricate jungle. Sometimes a spray of delicate foliage would be thrown out flat, the light lying flatly along the top of it, so that against a dark background it seemed almost luminous. There was a great bush over the thicket (for, indeed, it was more of a thicket than a wood); and the vague rumours that went among the tree-tops, and the occasional rustling of big birds or hares among the undergrowth, had in them a note of almost treacherous stealthiness, that put the imagination on its guard and made me walk warily on the russet carpeting of last year's leaves. The spirit of the place seemed to be all attention; the wood listened as I went, and held its breath to number my footfalls. One could not help feeling that there ought to be some reason for this stillness; whether, as the bright old legend goes, Pan lay somewhere near in siesta, or whether, perhaps, the heaven was meditating rain, and the first drops would soon come pattering through the leaves. It was not unpleasant, in such an humour, to catch sight, ever and anon, of large spaces of the open plain. This happened only where the path lay much upon the slope, and there was a flaw in the solid leafy thatch of the wood at some distance below the level at which I chanced myself to be walking; then, indeed, little scraps of foreshortened distance, miniature fields, and Lilliputian houses and hedgerow trees would appear for a moment in the aperture, and grow larger and smaller, and change and melt one into another, as I continued to go forward, and so shift my point of view.

For ten minutes, perhaps, I had heard from somewhere before me in the wood a strange, continuous noise, as of clucking, cooing, and gobbling, now and again interrupted by a harsh scream. As I advanced towards this noise, it began to grow lighter about me, and I caught sight, through the trees, of sundry gables and enclosure walls, and something like the tops of a rickyard. And sure enough, a rickyard it proved to be, and a neat little farm-steading, with the beech-woods growing almost to the door of it. Just before me, however, as I came upon the path, the trees drew back and let in a wide flood of daylight on to a circular lawn. It was here that the noises had their origin. More than a score of peacocks (there are altogether thirty at the farm), a proper contingent of peahens, and a great multitude that I could not number of more ordinary barn-door fowls, were all feeding together on this little open lawn among the beeches. They fed in a dense crowd, which swayed to and fro, and came hither and thither as by a sort of tide, and of which the surface was agitated like the surface of a sea as each bird guzzled his head along the ground after the scattered corn. The clucking, cooing noise that had led me thither was formed by the blending together of countless expressions of individual contentment into one collective expression of contentment, or general grace during meat. Every now and again a big peacock would separate himself from the mob and take a stately turn or two about the lawn, or perhaps mount for a moment upon the rail, and there shrilly publish to the world his satisfaction with himself and what he had to eat. It happened, for my sins, that none of these admirable birds had anything beyond the merest rudiment of a tail. Tails, it seemed, were out of season just then. But they had their necks for all that; and by their necks alone they do as much surpass all the other birds of our grey climate as they fall in quality of song below the blackbird or the lark. Surely the peacock, with its incomparable parade of glorious colour and the scannel voice of it issuing forth, as in mockery, from its painted throat, must, like my landlady's butterflies at Great Missenden, have been invented by some skilful fabulist for the consolation and support of homely virtue: or rather, perhaps, by a fabulist not quite so skilful, who made points for the moment without having a studious enough eye to the complete effect; for I thought these melting greens and blues so beautiful that afternoon, that I would have given them my vote just then before the sweetest pipe in all the spring woods. For indeed there is no piece of colour of the same extent in nature, that will so flatter and satisfy the lust of a man's eyes; and to come upon so many of them, after these acres of stone-coloured heavens and russet woods, and grey-brown ploughlands and white roads, was like going three whole days' journey to the southward, or a month back into the summer.

I was sorry to leave Peacock Farm—for so the place is called, after the name of its splendid pensioners—and go forwards again in the quiet woods. It began to grow both damp and dusk under the beeches; and as the day declined the colour faded out of the foliage; and shadow, without form and void, took the place of all the fine tracery of leaves and delicate gradations of living green that had before accompanied my walk. I had been sorry to leave Peacock Farm, but I was not sorry to find myself once more in the open road, under a pale and somewhat troubled-looking evening sky, and put my best foot foremost for the inn at Wendover.

Wendover, in itself, is a straggling, purposeless sort of place. Everybody seems to have had his own opinion as to how the street should go; or rather, every now and then a man seems to have arisen with a new idea on the subject, and led away a little sect of neighbours to join in his heresy. It would have somewhat the look of an abortive watering-place, such as we may now see them here and there along the coast, but for the age of the houses, the comely quiet design of some of them, and the look of long habitation, of a life that is settled and rooted, and makes it worth while to train flowers about the windows, and otherwise shape the dwelling to the humour of the inhabitant. The church, which might perhaps have served as rallying-point for these loose houses, and pulled the township into something like intelligible unity, stands some distance off among great trees; but the inn (to take the public buildings in order of importance) is in what I understand to be the principal street: a pleasant old house, with bay-windows, and three peaked gables, and many swallows' nests plastered about the eaves.

The interior of the inn was answerable to the outside: indeed, I never saw any room much more to be admired than the low wainscoted parlour in which I spent the remainder of the evening. It was a short oblong in shape, save that the fireplace was built across one of the angles so as to cut it partially off, and the opposite angle was similarly truncated by a corner cupboard. The wainscot was white, and there was a Turkey carpet on the floor, so old that it might have been imported by Walter Shandy before he retired, worn almost through in some places, but in others making a good show of blues and oranges, none the less harmonious for being somewhat faded. The corner cupboard was agreeable in design; and there were just the right things upon the shelves—decanters and tumblers, and blue plates, and one red rose in a glass of water. The furniture was old-fashioned and stiff. Everything was in keeping, down to the ponderous leaden inkstand on the round table. And you may fancy how pleasant it looked, all flushed and flickered over by the light of a brisk companionable fire, and seen, in a strange, tilted sort of perspective, in the three compartments of the old mirror above the chimney. As I sat reading in the great armchair, I kept looking round with the tail of my eye at the quaint, bright picture that was about me, and could not help some pleasure and a certain childish pride in forming part of it. The book I read was about Italy in the early Renaissance, the pageantries and the light loves of princes, the passion of men for learning, and poetry, and art; but it was written, by good luck, after a solid, prosaic fashion, that suited the room infinitely more nearly than the matter; and the result was that I thought less, perhaps, of Lippo Lippi, or Lorenzo, or Politian, than of the good Englishman who had written in that volume what he knew of them, and taken so much pleasure in his solemn polysyllables.

I was not left without society. My landlord had a very pretty little daughter, whom we shall call Lizzie. If I had made any notes at the time, I might be able to tell you something definite of her appearance. But faces have a trick of growing more and more spiritualised and abstract in the memory, until nothing remains of them but a look, a haunting expression; just that secret quality in a face that is apt to slip out somehow under the cunningest painter's touch, and leave the portrait dead for the lack of it. And if it is hard to catch with the finest of camel's-hair pencils, you may think how hopeless it must be to pursue after it with clumsy words. If I say, for instance, that this look, which I remember as Lizzie, was something wistful that seemed partly to come of slyness and in part of simplicity, and that I am inclined to imagine it had something to do with the daintiest suspicion of a cast in one of her large eyes, I shall have said all that I can, and the reader will not be much advanced towards comprehension. I had struck up an acquaintance with this little damsel in the morning, and professed much interest in her dolls, and an impatient desire to see the large one which was kept locked away for great occasions. And so I had not been very long in the parlour before the door opened, and in came Miss Lizzie with two dolls tucked clumsily under her arm. She was followed by her brother John, a year or so younger than herself, not simply to play propriety at our interview, but to show his own two whips in emulation of his sister's dolls. I did my best to make myself agreeable to my visitors, showing much admiration for the dolls and dolls' dresses, and, with a very serious demeanour, asking many questions about their age and character. I do not think that Lizzie distrusted my sincerity, but it was evident that she was both bewildered and a little contemptuous. Although she was ready herself to treat her dolls as if they were alive, she seemed to think rather poorly of any grown person who could fall heartily into the spirit of the fiction. Sometimes she would look at me with gravity and a sort of disquietude, as though she really feared I must be out of my wits. Sometimes, as when I inquired too particularly into the question of their names, she laughed at me so long and heartily that I began to feel almost embarrassed. But when, in an evil moment, I asked to be allowed to kiss one of them, she could keep herself no longer to herself. Clambering down from the chair on which she sat perched to show me, Cornelia-like, her jewels, she ran straight out of the room and into the bar—it was just across the passage,—and I could hear her telling her mother in loud tones, but apparently more in sorrow than in merriment, that *the gentleman in the parlour wanted to kiss Dolly.* I fancy she was determined to save me from this humiliating action, even in spite of myself, for she never gave me the desired permission. She reminded me of an old dog I once knew, who would never suffer the master of the house to dance, out of an exaggerated sense of the dignity of that master's place and carriage.

After the young people were gone there was but one more incident ere I went to bed. I heard a party of children go up and down the dark street for a while, singing together sweetly. And the mystery of this little incident was so pleasant to me that I purposely refrained from asking who they were, and wherefore they went singing at so late an hour. One can rarely be in a pleasant place without meeting with some pleasant accident. I have a conviction that these children would not have gone singing before the inn unless the inn-parlour had been the delightful place it was. At least, if I had been in the customary public room of the modern hotel, with all its disproportions and discomforts, my ears would have been dull, and there would have been some ugly temper or other uppermost in my spirit, and so they would have wasted their songs upon an unworthy hearer.

Next morning I went along to visit the church. It is a long-backed red-and-white building, very much restored, and stands in a pleasant graveyard among those great trees of which I have spoken already. The sky was drowned in a mist. Now and again pulses of cold wind went about the enclosure, and set the branches busy overhead, and the dead leaves scurrying into the angles of the church buttresses. Now and again, also, I could hear the dull sudden fall of a chestnut among the grass—the dog would bark before the rectory door—or there would come a clinking of pails from the stable-yard behind. But in spite of these occasional interruptions—in spite, also, of the continuous autumn twittering that filled the trees—the chief impression somehow was one as of utter silence, insomuch that the little greenish bell that peeped out of a window in the tower disquieted me with a sense of some possible and more inharmonious disturbance. The grass was wet, as if with a hoar frost that had just been melted. I do not know that ever I saw a morning more autumnal. As I went to and fro among the graves, I saw some flowers set reverently before a recently erected tomb, and drawing near, was almost startled to find they lay on the grave a man seventy-two years old when he died. We are accustomed to strew flowers only over the young, where love has been cut short untimely, and great possibilities have been restrained by death. We strew them there in token, that these possibilities, in some deeper sense, shall yet be realised, and the touch of our dead loves remain with us and guide us to the end. And yet there was more significance, perhaps, and perhaps a greater consolation, in this little nosegay on the grave of one who had died old. We are apt to make so much of the tragedy of death, and think so little of the enduring tragedy of some men's lives, that we see more to lament for in a life cut off in the midst of usefulness and love, than in one that miserably survives all love and usefulness, and goes about the world the phantom of itself, without hope, or joy, or any consolation. These flowers seemed not so much the token of love that survived death, as of something yet more beautiful—of love that had lived a man's life out to an end with him, and been faithful and companionable, and not weary of loving, throughout all these years.

The morning cleared a little, and the sky was once more the old stone-coloured vault over the sallow meadows and the russet woods, as I set forth on a dog-cart from Wendover to Tring. The road lay for a good distance along the side of the hills, with the great plain below on one hand, and the beech-woods above on the other. The fields were busy with people ploughing and sowing; every here and there a jug of ale stood in the angle of the hedge, and I could see many a team wait smoking in the furrow as ploughman or sower stepped aside for a moment to take a draught. Over all the brown ploughlands, and under all the leafless hedgerows, there was a stout piece of labour abroad, and, as it were, a spirit of picnic. The horses smoked and the men laboured and shouted and drank in the sharp autumn morning; so that one had a strong effect of large, open-air existence. The fellow who drove me was something of a humourist; and his conversation was all in praise of an agricultural labourer's way of life. It was he who called my attention to these jugs of ale by the hedgerow; he could not sufficiently express the liberality of these men's wages; he told me how sharp an appetite was given by breaking up the earth in the morning air, whether with plough or spade, and cordially admired this provision of nature. He sang O fortunatos agricolas! indeed, in every possible key, and with many cunning inflections, till I began to wonder what was the use of such people as Mr. Arch, and to sing the same air myself in a more diffident manner.

Tring was reached, and then Tring railway-station; for the two are not very near, the good people of Tring having held the railway, of old days, in extreme apprehension, lest some day it should break loose in the town and work mischief. I had a last walk, among russet beeches as usual, and the air filled, as usual, with the carolling of larks; I heard shots fired in the distance, and saw, as a new sign of the fulfilled autumn, two horsemen exercising a pack of fox-hounds. And then the train came and carried me back to London.

CHAPTER IV—A WINTER'S WALK IN CARRICK AND GALLOWAY—A FRAGMENT—1876

At the famous bridge of Doon, Kyle, the central district of the shire of Ayr, marches with Carrick, the most southerly. On the Carrick side of the river rises a hill of somewhat gentle conformation, cleft with shallow dells, and sown here and there with farms and tufts of wood. Inland, it loses itself, joining, I suppose, the great herd of similar hills that occupies the centre of the Lowlands. Towards the sea it swells out the coast-line into a protuberance, like a bay-window in a plan, and is fortified against the surf behind bold crags. This hill is known as the Brown Hill of Carrick, or, more shortly, Brown Carrick.

It had snowed overnight. The fields were all sheeted up; they were tucked in among the snow, and their shape was modelled through the pliant counterpane, like children tucked in by a fond mother. The wind had made ripples and folds upon the surface, like what the sea, in quiet weather, leaves upon the sand. There was a frosty stifle in the air. An effusion of coppery light on the summit of Brown Carrick showed where the sun was trying to look through; but along the horizon clouds of cold fog had settled down, so that there was no distinction of sky and sea. Over the white shoulders of the headlands, or in the opening of bays, there was nothing but a great vacancy and blackness; and the road as it drew near the edge of the cliff seemed to skirt the shores of creation and void space.

The snow crunched under foot, and at farms all the dogs broke out barking as they smelt a passer-by upon the road. I met a fine old fellow, who might have sat as the father in 'The Cottar's Saturday Night,' and who swore most heathenishly at a cow he was driving. And a little after I scraped acquaintance with a poor body tramping out to gather cockles. His face was wrinkled by exposure; it was broken up into flakes and channels, like mud beginning to dry, and weathered in two colours, an incongruous pink and grey. He had a faint air of being surprised—which, God knows, he might well be—that life had gone so ill with him. The shape of his trousers was in itself a jest, so strangely were they bagged and ravelled about his knees; and his coat was all bedaubed with clay as tough he had lain in a rain-dub during the New Year's festivity. I will own I was not sorry to think he had had a merry New Year, and been young again for an evening; but I was sorry to see the mark still there. One could not expect such an old gentleman to be much of a dandy or a great student of respectability in dress; but there might have been a wife at home, who had brushed out similar stains after fifty New Years, now become old, or a round-armed daughter, who would wish to have him neat, were it only out of self-respect and for the ploughman sweetheart when he looks round at night. Plainly, there was nothing of this in his life, and years and loneliness hung heavily on his old arms. He was seventy-six, he told me; and nobody would give a day's work to a man that age: they would think he couldn't do it. 'And, 'deed,' he went on, with a sad little chuckle, "'deed, I doubt if I could.' He said goodbye to me at a footpath, and crippled wearily off to his work. It will make your heart ache if you think of his old fingers groping in the snow.

He told me I was to turn down beside the school-house for Dunure. And so, when I found a lone house among the snow, and heard a babble of childish voices from within, I struck off into a steep road leading downwards to the sea. Dunure lies close under the steep hill: a haven among the rocks, a breakwater in consummate disrepair, much apparatus for drying nets, and a score or so of fishers' houses. Hard by, a few shards of ruined castle overhang the sea, a few vaults, and one tall gable honeycombed with windows. The snow lay on the beach to the tidemark. It was daubed on to the sills of the ruin: it roosted in the crannies of the rock like white sea-birds; even on outlying reefs there would be a little cock of snow, like a toy lighthouse. Everything was grey and white in a cold and dolorous sort of shepherd's plaid. In the profound silence, broken only by the noise of oars at sea, a horn was sounded twice; and I saw the postman, girt with two bags, pause a moment at the end of the clachan for letters.

It is, perhaps, characteristic of Dunure that none were brought him.

The people at the public-house did not seem well pleased to see me, and though I would fain have stayed by the kitchen fire, sent me 'ben the hoose' into the guest-room. This guest-room at Dunure was painted in quite aesthetic fashion. There are rooms in the same taste not a hundred miles from London, where persons of an extreme sensibility meet together without embarrassment. It was all in a fine dull bottle-green and black; a grave harmonious piece of colouring, with nothing, so far as coarser folk can judge, to hurt the better feelings of the most exquisite purist. A cherry-red half window-blind kept up an imaginary warmth in the cold room, and threw quite a glow on the floor. Twelve cockle-shells and a half-penny china figure were ranged solemnly along the mantel-shelf. Even the spittoon was an original note, and instead of sawdust contained sea-shells. And as for the hearthrug, it would merit an article to itself, and a coloured diagram to help the text. It was patch-work, but the patchwork of the poor; no glowing shreds of old brocade and Chinese silk, shaken together in the kaleidoscope of some tasteful housewife's fancy; but a work of art in its own way, and plainly a la-bour of love. The patches came exclusively from people's raiment. There was no colour more brilliant than a heather mixture; 'My Johnny's grey breeks,' well polished over the oar on the boat's thwart, entered largely into its composition. And the spoils of an old black cloth coat, that had been many a Sunday to church, added something (save the mark!) of preciousness to the material.

While I was at luncheon four carters came in—long-limbed, mus-cular Ayrshire Scots, with lean, intelligent faces. Four quarts of stout were ordered; they kept filling the tumbler with the other hand as they drank; and in less time than it takes me to write these words the four quarts were finished—another round was proposed, discussed, and neg-atived—and they were creaking out of the village with their carts.

The ruins drew you towards them. You never saw any place more desolate from a distance, nor one that less belied its promise near at hand. Some crows and gulls flew away croaking as I scrambled in. The snow had drifted into the vaults. The clachan dabbled with snow, the white hills, the black sky, the sea marked in the coves with faint circular wrinkles, the whole world, as it looked from a loop-hole in Dunure, was cold, wretched, and out-at-elbows. If you had been a wicked baron and compelled to stay there all the afternoon, you would have had a rare fit of remorse. How you would have heaped up the fire and gnawed your fingers! I think it would have come to homicide before the evening—if it were only for the pleasure of seeing something red! And the masters of Dunure, it is to be noticed, were remarkable of old for inhumanity. One of these vaults where the snow had drifted was that 'black route' where 'Mr. Alane Stewart, Commendatour of Crossraguel,' endured his fiery trials. On the 1st and 7th of September 1570 (ill dates for Mr. Alan!),

Gilbert, Earl of Cassilis, his chaplain, his baker, his cook, his pantry-man, and another servant, bound the Poor Commendator 'betwix an iron chimlay and a fire,' and there cruelly roasted him until he signed away his abbacy. it is one of the ugliest stories of an ugly period, but not, somehow, without such a flavour of the ridiculous as makes it hard to sympathise quite seriously with the victim. And it is consoling to remember that he got away at last, and kept his abbacy, and, over and above, had a pension from the Earl until he died.

Some way beyond Dunure a wide bay, of somewhat less unkindly aspect, opened out. Colzean plantations lay all along the steep shore, and there was a wooded hill towards the centre, where the trees made a sort of shadowy etching over the snow. The road went down and up, and past a blacksmith's cottage that made fine music in the valley. Three compatriots of Burns drove up to me in a cart. They were all drunk, and asked me jeeringly if this was the way to Dunure. I told them it was; and my answer was received with unfeigned merriment. One gentleman was so much tickled he nearly fell out of the cart; indeed, he was only saved by a companion, who either had not so fine a sense of humour or had drunken less.

'The toune of Mayboll,' says the inimitable Abercrummie,[3] 'stands upon an ascending ground from east to west, and lyes open to the south. It hath one principals street, with houses upon both sides, built of free-stone; and it is beautifyed with the situation of two castles, one at each end of this street. That on the east belongs to the Erle of Cassilis. On the west end is a castle, which belonged sometime to the laird of Blair-quan, which is now the tolbuith, and is adorned with a pyremide [conical roof], and a row of ballesters round it raised from the top of the staircase, into which they have mounted a fyne clock. There be four lanes which pass from the principall street; one is called the Black Vennel, which is steep, declining to the south-west, and leads to a lower street, which is far larger than the high chiefe street, and it runs from the Kirkland to the Well Trees, in which there have been many pretty buildings, be-longing to the severall gentry of the countrey, who were wont to resort thither in winter, and divert themselves in converse together at their owne houses. It was once the principall street of the town; but many of these houses of the gentry having been decayed and ruined, it has lost much of its ancient beautie. Just opposite to this vennel, there is another that leads north-west, from the chiefe street to the green, which is a pleasant plott of ground, enclosed round with an earthen wall, wherein

3   William Abercrombie. See *Fasti Ecclesia Scoticanae*, under 'Maybole' (Part iii.).

they were wont to play football, but now at the Gowff and byasse-bowls. The houses of this towne, on both sides of the street, have their several gardens belonging to them; and in the lower street there be some pretty orchards, that yield store of good fruit.' As Patterson says, this description is near enough even to-day, and is mighty nicely written to boot. I am bound to add, of my own experience, that Maybole is tumbledown and dreary. Prosperous enough in reality, it has an air of decay; and though the population has increased, a roofless house every here and there seems to protest the contrary. The women are more than well-favoured, and the men fine tall fellows; but they look slipshod and dissipated. As they slouched at street corners, or stood about gossiping in the snow, it seemed they would have been more at home in the slums of a large city than here in a country place betwixt a village and a town. I heard a great deal about drinking, and a great deal about religious revivals: two things in which the Scottish character is emphatic and most unlovely. In particular, I heard of clergymen who were employing their time in explaining to a delighted audience the physics of the Second Coming. It is not very likely any of us will be asked to help. if we were, it is likely we should receive instructions for the occasion, and that on more reliable authority. And so I can only figure to myself a congregation truly curious in such flights of theological fancy, as one of veteran and accomplished saints, who have fought the good fight to an end and outlived all worldly passion, and are to be regarded rather as a part of the Church Triumphant than the poor, imperfect company on earth. And yet I saw some young fellows about the smoking-room who seemed, in the eyes of one who cannot count himself strait-laced, in need of some more practical sort of teaching. They seemed only eager to get drunk, and to do so speedily. It was not much more than a week after the New Year; and to hear them return on their past bouts with a gusto unspeakable was not altogether pleasing. Here is one snatch of talk, for the accuracy of which I can vouch—

'Ye had a spree here last Tuesday?'

'We had that!'

'I wasna able to be oot o' my bed. Man, I was awful bad on Wednesday.'

'Ay, ye were gey bad.'

And you should have seen the bright eyes, and heard the sensual accents! They recalled their doings with devout gusto and a sort of rational pride. Schoolboys, after their first drunkenness, are not more boastful; a cock does not plume himself with a more unmingled satisfaction as he paces forth among his harem; and yet these were grown men, and by no means short of wit. It was hard to suppose they were very eager about the Second Coming: it seemed as if some elementary notions of temperance for the men and seemliness for the women would have gone nearer the mark. And yet, as it seemed to me typical of much that is evil in Scotland, Maybole is also typical of much that is best. Some of the factories, which have taken the place of weaving in the town's economy, were originally founded and are still possessed by self-made men of the sterling, stout old breed—fellows who made some little bit of an invention, borrowed some little pocketful of capital, and then, step by step, in courage, thrift and industry, fought their way upwards to an assured position.

Abercrummie has told you enough of the Tolbooth; but, as a bit of spelling, this inscription on the Tolbooth bell seems too delicious to withhold: 'This bell is founded at Maiboll Bi Danel Geli, a Frenchman, the 6th November, 1696, Bi appointment of the heritors of the parish of Maiyboll.' The Castle deserves more notice. It is a large and shapely tower, plain from the ground upwards, but with a zone of ornamentation running about the top. In a general way this adornment is perched on the very summit of the chimney-stacks; but there is one corner more elaborate than the rest. A very heavy string-course runs round the upper story, and just above this, facing up the street, the tower carries a small oriel window, fluted and corbelled and carved about with stone heads. It is so ornate it has somewhat the air of a shrine. And it was, indeed, the casket of a very precious jewel, for in the room to which it gives light lay, for long years, the heroine of the sweet old ballad of 'Johnnie Faa'—she who, at the call of the gipsies' songs, 'came tripping down the stair, and all her maids before her.' Some people say the ballad has no basis in fact, and have written, I believe, unanswerable papers to the proof. But in the face of all that, the very look of that high oriel window convinces the imagination, and we enter into all the sorrows of the imprisoned dame. We conceive the burthen of the long, lack-lustre days, when she leaned her sick head against the mullions, and saw the burghers loafing in Maybole High Street, and the children at play, and ruffling gallants riding by from hunt or foray. We conceive the passion of odd moments, when the wind threw up to her some snatch of song, and her heart grew hot within her, and her eyes overflowed at the memory of the past. And even if the tale be not true of this or that lady, or this or that old tower, it is true in the essence of all men and women: for all of us, some time or other, hear the gipsies singing; over all of us is the glamour cast. Some resist and sit resolutely by the fire. Most go and are brought back again, like Lady Cassilis. A few, of the tribe of Waring, go and are seen no more; only now and again, at springtime, when the gipsies' song is afloat in the amethyst evening, we can catch their voices in the glee.

By night it was clearer, and Maybole more visible than during the day. Clouds coursed over the sky in great masses; the full moon battled the other way, and lit up the snow with gleams of flying silver; the town came down the hill in a cascade of brown gables, bestridden by smooth white roofs, and sprangled here and there with lighted windows. At either end the snow stood high up in the darkness, on the peak of the Tolbooth and among the chimneys of the Castle. As the moon flashed a bull's-eye glitter across the town between the racing clouds, the white roofs leaped into relief over the gables and the chimney-stacks, and their shadows over the white roofs. In the town itself the lit face of the clock peered down the street; an hour was hammered out on Mr. Geli's bell, and from behind the red curtains of a public-house some one trolled out—a compatriot of Burns, again!—'The saut tear blin's my e'e.'

Next morning there was sun and a flapping wind. From the street corners of Maybole I could catch breezy glimpses of green fields. The road underfoot was wet and heavy—part ice, part snow, part water, and any one I met greeted me, by way of salutation, with 'A fine thowe' (thaw). My way lay among rather bleak bills, and past bleak ponds and dilapidated castles and monasteries, to the Highland-looking village of Kirkoswald. It has little claim to notice, save that Burns came there to study surveying in the summer of 1777, and there also, in the kirkyard, the original of Tam o' Shanter sleeps his last sleep. It is worth notic-ing, however, that this was the first place I thought 'Highland-looking.' Over the bill from Kirkoswald a farm-road leads to the coast. As I came down above Turnberry, the sea view was indeed strangely different from the day before. The cold fogs were all blown away; and there was Ailsa Craig, like a refraction, magnified and deformed, of the Bass Rock; and there were the chiselled mountain-tops of Arran, veined and tipped with snow; and behind, and fainter, the low, blue land of Cantyre. Cot-tony clouds stood in a great castle over the top of Arran, and blew out in long streamers to the south. The sea was bitten all over with white; little ships, tacking up and down the Firth, lay over at different angles in the wind. On Shanter they were ploughing lea; a cart foal, all in a field by himself, capered and whinnied as if the spring were in him.

The road from Turnberry to Girvan lies along the shore, among sand-hills and by wildernesses of tumbled bent. Every here and there a few cottages stood together beside a bridge. They had one odd feature, not easy to describe in words: a triangular porch projected from above the door, supported at the apex by a single upright post; a secondary door was hinged to the post, and could be hasped on either cheek of the real entrance; so, whether the wind was north or south, the cotter could make himself a triangular bight of shelter where to set his chair and finish a pipe with comfort. There is one objection to this device; for, as the post stands in the middle of the fairway, any one precipitately issuing from the cottage must run his chance of a broken head. So far as I am aware, it is peculiar to the little corner of country about Girvan. And that corner is noticeable for more reasons: it is certainly one of the most characteristic districts in Scotland, It has this movable porch by way of architecture; it has, as we shall see, a sort of remnant of provincial costume, and it has the handsomest population in the Lowlands. . . .

CHAPTER V—FOREST NOTES 1875-6

On the Plain

Perhaps the reader knows already the aspect of the great levels of the Gatinais, where they border with the wooded hills of Fontainebleau. Here and there a few grey rocks creep out of the forest as if to sun themselves. Here and there a few apple-trees stand together on a knoll. The quaint, undignified tartan of a myriad small fields dies out into the distance; the strips blend and disappear; and the dead flat lies forth open and empty, with no accident save perhaps a thin line of trees or faint church spire against the sky. Solemn and vast at all times, in spite of pettiness in the near details, the impression becomes more solemn and vast towards evening. The sun goes down, a swollen orange, as it were into the sea. A blue-clad peasant rides home, with a harrow smoking behind him among the dry clods. Another still works with his wife in their little strip. An immense shadow fills the plain; these people stand in it up to their shoulders; and their heads, as they stoop over their work and rise again, are relieved from time to time against the golden sky.

These peasant farmers are well off nowadays, and not by any means overworked; but somehow you always see in them the historical representative of the serf of yore, and think not so much of present times, which may be prosperous enough, as of the old days when the peasant was taxed beyond possibility of payment, and lived, in Michelet's image, like a hare between two furrows. These very people now weeding their patch under the broad sunset, that very man and his wife, it seems to us, have suffered all the wrongs of France. It is they who have been their country's scapegoat for long ages; they who, generation after generation, have sowed and not reaped, reaped and another has garnered; and who have now entered into their reward, and enjoy their good things in their turn. For the days are gone by when the Seigneur ruled and profited. 'Le

Seigneur,' says the old formula, 'enferme ses manants comme sous porte et gonds, du ciel à la terre. Tout est à lui, foret chenue, oiseau dans l'air, poisson dans l'eau, bete an buisson, l'onde qui coule, la cloche dont le son au loin roule.' Such was his old state of sovereignty, a local god rather than a mere king. And now you may ask yourself where he is, and look round for vestiges of my late lord, and in all the country-side there is no trace of him but his forlorn and fallen mansion. At the end of a long avenue, now sown with grain, in the midst of a close full of cypresses and lilacs, ducks and crowing chanticleers and droning bees, the old chateau lifts its red chimneys and peaked roofs and turning vanes into the wind and sun. There is a glad spring bustle in the air, perhaps, and the lilacs are all in flower, and the creepers green about the broken balustrade: but no spring shall revive the honour of the place. Old women of the people, little, children of the people, saunter and gambol in the walled court or feed the ducks in the neglected moat. Plough-horses, mighty of limb, browse in the long stables. The dial-hand on the clock waits for some better hour. Out on the plain, where hot sweat trickles into men's eyes, and the spade goes in deep and comes up slowly, perhaps the peasant may feel a movement of joy at his heart when he thinks that these spacious chimneys are now cold, which have so often blazed and flickered upon gay folk at supper, while he and his hollow-eyed children watched through the night with empty bellies and cold feet. And perhaps, as he raises his head and sees the forest lying like a coast-line of low hills along the sea-level of the plain, perhaps forest and chateau hold no unsimilar place in his affections.

If the chateau was my lord's, the forest was my lord the king's; neither of them for this poor Jacques. If he thought to eke out his meagre way of life by some petty theft of wood for the fire, or for a new roof-tree, he found himself face to face with a whole department, from the Grand Master of the Woods and Waters, who was a high-born lord, down to the common sergeant, who was a peasant like himself, and wore stripes or a bandoleer by way of uniform. For the first offence, by the Salic law, there was a fine of fifteen sols; and should a man be taken more than once in fault, or circumstances aggravate the colour of his guilt, he might be whipped, branded, or hanged. There was a hangman over at Melun, and, I doubt not, a fine tall gibbet hard by the town gate, where Jacques might see his fellows dangle against the sky as he went to market.

And then, if he lived near to a cover, there would be the more hares and rabbits to eat out his harvest, and the more hunters to trample it down. My lord has a new horn from England. He has laid out seven francs in decorating it with silver and gold, and fitting it with a silken leash to hang about his shoulder. The hounds have been on a pilgrimage to the shrine of Saint Mesmer, or Saint Hubert in the Ardennes, or some other holy intercessor who has made a speciality of the health of hunting-dogs. In the grey dawn the game was turned and the branch broken by our best piqueur. A rare day's hunting lies before us. Wind a jolly flourish, sound the bien-aller with all your lungs. Jacques must stand by, hat in hand, while the quarry and hound and huntsman sweep across his field, and a year's sparing and labouring is as though it had not been. If he can see the ruin with a good enough grace, who knows but he may fall in favour with my lord; who knows but his son may become the last and least among the servants at his lordship's kennel—one of the two poor varlets who get no wages and sleep at night among the hounds? [4]

For all that, the forest has been of use to Jacques, not only warming him with fallen wood, but giving him shelter in days of sore trouble, when my lord of the chateau, with all his troopers and trumpets, had been beaten from field after field into some ultimate fastness, or lay over-seas in an English prison. In these dark days, when the watch on the church steeple saw the smoke of burning villages on the sky-line, or a clump of spears and fluttering pensions drawing nigh across the plain, these good folk gat them up, with all their household gods, into the wood, whence, from some high spur, their timid scouts might overlook the coming and going of the marauders, and see the harvest ridden down, and church and cottage go up to heaven all night in flame. It was but an unhomely refuge that the woods afforded, where they must abide all change of weather and keep house with wolves and vipers. Often there was none left alive, when they returned, to show the old divisions of field from field. And yet, as times went, when the wolves entered at night into depopulated Paris, and perhaps De Retz was passing by with a company of demons like himself, even in these caves and thickets there were glad hearts and grateful prayers.

Once or twice, as I say, in the course of the ages, the forest may have served the peasant well, but at heart it is a royal forest, and noble by old associations. These woods have rung to the horns of all the kings of France, from Philip Augustus downwards. They have seen Saint Louis exercise the dogs he brought with him from Egypt; Francis I. go

---

4   'Duex poures varlez qui n'ont nulz gages et qui gissoient la nuit avec les chiens.' See Champollion—Figeac's *Louis et Charles d'Orléans*, i. 63, and for my lord's English horn, *ibid.* 96.

a-hunting with ten thousand horses in his train; and Peter of Russia following his first stag. And so they are still haunted for the imagination by royal hunts and progresses, and peopled with the faces of memorable men of yore. And this distinction is not only in virtue of the pastime of dead monarchs.

Great events, great revolutions, great cycles in the affairs of men, have here left their note, here taken shape in some significant and dramatic situation. It was hence that Gruise and his leaguers led Charles the Ninth a prisoner to Paris. Here, booted and spurred, and with all his dogs about him, Napoleon met the Pope beside a woodland cross. Here, on his way to Elba not so long after, he kissed the eagle of the Old Guard, and spoke words of passionate farewell to his soldiers. And here, after Waterloo, rather than yield its ensign to the new power, one of his faithful regiments burned that memorial of so much toil and glory on the Grand Master's table, and drank its dust in brandy, as a devout priest consumes the remnants of the Host.

In the Season

Close into the edge of the forest, so close that the trees of the bornage stand pleasantly about the last houses, sits a certain small and very quiet village. There is but one street, and that, not long ago, was a green lane, where the cattle browsed between the doorsteps. As you go up this street, drawing ever nearer the beginning of the wood, you will arrive at last before an inn where artists lodge. To the door (for I imagine it to be six o'clock on some fine summer's even), half a dozen, or maybe half a score, of people have brought out chairs, and now sit sunning themselves, and waiting the omnibus from Melun. If you go on into the court you will find as many more, some in billiard-room over absinthe and a match of corks some without over a last cigar and a vermouth. The doves coo and flutter from the dovecot; Hortense is drawing water from the well; and as all the rooms open into the court, you can see the white-capped cook over the furnace in the kitchen, and some idle painter, who has stored his canvases and washed his brushes, jangling a waltz on the crazy, tongue-tied piano in the salle-à-manger. 'Edmond, encore un vermouth,' cries a man in velveteen, adding in a tone of apologetic afterthought, 'un double, s'il vous plaît.' 'Where are you working?' asks one in pure white linen from top to toe. 'At the Carrefour de l'Épine,' returns the other in corduroy (they are all gaitered, by the way). 'I couldn't do a thing to it. I ran out of white. Where were you?' 'I wasn't working. I was looking for motives.' Here is an outbreak of jubilation, and a lot of men clustering together about some new-comer with outstretched hands; perhaps the 'correspondence' has come in and brought So-and-so from Paris, or perhaps it is only So-and-so who has walked over from Chailly to dinner.

'À table, Messieurs!' cries M. Siron, bearing through the court the first tureen of soup. And immediately the company begins to settle down about the long tables in the dining-room, framed all round with sketches of all degrees of merit and demerit. There's the big picture of the huntsman winding a horn with a dead boar between his legs, and his legs—well, his legs in stockings. And here is the little picture of a raw mutton-chop, in which Such-a-one knocked a hole last summer with no worse a missile than a plum from the dessert. And under all these works of art so much eating goes forward, so much drinking, so much jabbering in French and English, that it would do your heart good merely to peep and listen at the door. One man is telling how they all went last year to the fete at Fleury, and another how well so-and-so would sing of an evening: and here are a third and fourth making plans for the whole future of their lives; and there is a fifth imitating a conjurer and making faces on his clenched fist, surely of all arts the most difficult and admirable! A sixth has eaten his fill, lights a cigarette, and resigns himself to digestion. A seventh has just dropped in, and calls for soup. Number eight, meanwhile, has left the table, and is once more trampling the poor piano under powerful and uncertain fingers.

Dinner over, people drop outside to smoke and chat. Perhaps we go along to visit our friends at the other end of the village, where there is always a good welcome and a good talk, and perhaps some pickled oysters and white wine to close the evening. Or a dance is organised in the dining-room, and the piano exhibits all its paces under manful jockeying, to the light of three or four candles and a lamp or two, while the waltzers move to and fro upon the wooden floor, and sober men, who are not given to such light pleasures, get up on the table or the sideboard, and sit there looking on approvingly over a pipe and a tumbler of wine. Or sometimes—suppose my lady moon looks forth, and the court from out the half-lit dining-room seems nearly as bright as by day, and the light picks out the window-panes, and makes a clear shadow under every vine-leaf on the wall—sometimes a picnic is proposed, and a basket made ready, and a good procession formed in front of the hotel. The two trumpeters in honour go before; and as we file down the long alley, and up through devious footpaths among rocks and pine-trees, with every here and there a dark passage of shadow, and every here and there a spacious outlook over moonlit woods, these two precede us and sound many a jolly flourish as they walk. We gather ferns and dry boughs into the cavern, and soon a good blaze flutters the shadows of the old bandits' haunt, and shows shapely beards and comely faces and toilettes ranged about the wall. The bowl is lit, and the punch is burnt and sent round in scalding thimblefuls. So a good hour or two may pass with song and jest. And then we go home in the moonlit morning, straggling a good deal among the birch tufts and the boulders, but ever called together again, as one of our leaders winds his horn. Perhaps some one of the party will not heed the summons, but chooses out some by-way of his own. As he follows the winding sandy road, he hears the flourishes grow fainter and fainter in the distance, and die finally out, and still walks on in the strange coolness and silence and between the crisp lights and shadows of the moonlit woods, until suddenly the bell rings out the hour from far-away Chailly, and he starts to find himself alone. No surf-bell on forlorn and perilous shores, no passing knell over the busy market-place, can speak with a more heavy and disconsolate tongue to human ears. Each stroke calls up a host of ghostly reverberations in his mind. And as he stands rooted, it has grown once more so utterly silent that it seems to him he might hear the church bells ring the hour out all the world over, not at Chailly only, but in Paris, and away in outlandish cities, and in the village on the river, where his childhood passed between the sun and flowers.

Idle Hours

The woods by night, in all their uncanny effect, are not rightly to be understood until you can compare them with the woods by day. The stillness of the medium, the floor of glittering sand, these trees that go streaming up like monstrous sea-weeds and waver in the moving winds like the weeds in submarine currents, all these set the mind working on the thought of what you may have seen off a foreland or over the side of a boat, and make you feel like a diver, down in the quiet water, fathoms below the tumbling, transitory surface of the sea. And yet in itself, as I say, the strangeness of these nocturnal solitudes is not to be felt fully without the sense of contrast. You must have risen in the morning and seen the woods as they are by day, kindled and coloured in the sun's light; you must have felt the odour of innumerable trees at even, the unsparing heat along the forest roads, and the coolness of the groves.

And on the first morning you will doubtless rise betimes. If you have not been wakened before by the visit of some adventurous pigeon, you will be wakened as soon as the sun can reach your window—for there are no blind or shutters to keep him out—and the room, with its bare wood floor and bare whitewashed walls, shines all round you in a sort of glory of reflected lights. You may doze a while longer by snatches, or lie awake to study the charcoal men and dogs and horses with which former occupants have defiled the partitions: Thiers, with wily profile; local celebrities, pipe in hand; or, maybe, a romantic landscape splashed in oil. Meanwhile artist after artist drops into the salle-à-manger for coffee, and then shoulders easel, sunshade, stool, and paint-box, bound into a fagot, and sets of for what he calls his 'motive.' And artist after artist, as he goes out of the village, carries with him a little following of dogs. For the dogs, who belong only nominally to any special master, hang about the gate of the forest all day long, and whenever any one goes by who hits their fancy, profit by his escort, and go forth with him to play an hour or two at hunting. They would like to be under the trees all day. But they cannot go alone. They require a pretext. And so they take the passing artist as an excuse to go into the woods, as they might take a walking-stick as an excuse to bathe. With quick ears, long spines, and bandy legs, or perhaps as tall as a greyhound and with a bulldog's head, this company of mongrels will trot by your side all day and come home with you at night, still showing white teeth and wagging stunted tail. Their good humour is not to be exhausted. You may pelt them with stones if you please, and all they will do is to give you a wider berth. If once they come out with you, to you they will remain faithful, and with you return; although if you meet them next morning in the street, it is as like as not they will cut you with a countenance of brass.

The forest—a strange thing for an Englishman—is very destitute of birds. This is no country where every patch of wood among the meadows gibes up an increase of song, and every valley wandered through by a streamlet rings and reverberates from side to with a profusion of clear notes. And this rarity of birds is not to be regretted on its own account only. For the insects prosper in their absence, and become as one of the plagues of Egypt. Ants swarm in the hot sand; mosquitos drone their nasal drone; wherever the sun finds a hole in the roof of the forest, you see a myriad transparent creatures coming and going in the shaft of light; and even between-whiles, even where there is no incursion of sunrays into the dark arcade of the wood, you are conscious of a continual drift of insects, an ebb and flow of infinitesimal living things between the trees. Nor are insects the only evil creatures that haunt the forest. For you may plump into a cave among the rocks, and find yourself face to face with a wild boar, or see a crooked viper slither across the road.

Perhaps you may set yourself down in the bay between two spreading beech-roots with a book on your lap, and be awakened all of a sudden by a friend: 'I say, just keep where you are, will you? You make the jolliest motive.' And you reply: 'Well, I don't mind, if I may smoke.' And thereafter the hours go idly by. Your friend at the easel labours doggedly a little way off, in the wide shadow of the tree; and yet farther, across a strait of glaring sunshine, you see another painter, encamped in the shadow of another tree, and up to his waist in the fern. You cannot watch your own effigy growing out of the white trunk, and the trunk beginning to stand forth from the rest of the wood, and the whole picture getting dappled over with the flecks of sun that slip through the leaves overhead, and, as a wind goes by and sets the trees a-talking, flicker hither and thither like butterflies of light. But you know it is going forward; and, out of emulation with the painter, get ready your own palette, and lay out the colour for a woodland scene in words.

Your tree stands in a hollow paved with fern and heather, set in a basin of low hills, and scattered over with rocks and junipers. All the open is steeped in pitiless sunlight. Everything stands out as though it were cut in cardboard, every colour is strained into its highest key. The boulders are some of them upright and dead like monolithic castles, some of them prone like sleeping cattle. The junipers—looking, in their soiled and ragged mourning, like some funeral procession that has gone seeking the place of sepulchre three hundred years and more in wind and rain—are daubed in forcibly against the glowing ferns and heather. Every tassel of their rusty foliage is defined with pre-Raphaelite minuteness. And a sorry figure they make out there in the sun, like misbegotten yew-trees! The scene is all pitched in a key of colour so peculiar, and lit up with such a discharge of violent sunlight, as a man might live fifty years in England and not see.

Meanwhile at your elbow some one tunes up a song, words of Ronsard to a pathetic tremulous air, of how the poet loved his mistress long ago, and pressed on her the flight of time, and told her how white and quiet the dead lay under the stones, and how the boat dipped and pitched as the shades embarked for the passionless land. Yet a little while, sang the poet, and there shall be no more love; only to sit and remember loves that might have been. There is a falling flourish in the air that remains in the memory and comes back in incongruous places, on the seat of hansoms or in the warm bed at night, with something of a forest savour.

'You can get up now,' says the painter; 'I'm at the background.'

And so up you get, stretching yourself, and go your way into the wood, the daylight becoming richer and more golden, and the shadows stretching farther into the open. A cool air comes along the highways, and the scents awaken. The fir-trees breathe abroad their ozone. Out of unknown thickets comes forth the soft, secret, aromatic odour of the woods, not like a smell of the free heaven, but as though court ladies, who had known these paths in ages long gone by, still walked in the summer evenings, and shed from their brocades a breath of musk or bergamot upon the woodland winds. One side of the long avenues is still kindled with the sun, the other is plunged in transparent shadow. Over the trees the west begins to burn like a furnace; and the painters gather up their chattels, and go down, by avenue or footpath, to the plain.

A Pleasure-Party

As this excursion is a matter of some length, and, moreover, we go in force, we have set aside our usual vehicle, the pony-cart, and ordered a large wagonette from Lejosne's. It has been waiting for near an hour, while one went to pack a knapsack, and t'other hurried over his toilette and coffee; but now it is filled from end to end with merry folk in summer attire, the coachman cracks his whip, and amid much applause from round the inn door off we rattle at a spanking trot. The way lies through the forest, up hill and down dale, and by beech and pine wood, in the cheerful morning sunshine. The English get down at all the ascents and walk on ahead for exercise; the French are mightily entertained at this, and keep coyly underneath the tilt. As we go we carry with us a pleasant noise of laughter and light speech, and some one will be always breaking out into a bar or two of opera bouffe. Before we get to the Route Ronde here comes Desprez, the colourman from Fontainebleau, trudging across on his weekly peddle with a case of merchandise; and it is 'Desprez, leave me some malachite green'; 'Desprez, leave me so much canvas'; 'Desprez, leave me this, or leave me that'; M. Desprez standing the while in the sunlight with grave face and many salutations. The next interruption is more important. For some time back we have had the

sound of cannon in our ears; and now, a little past Franchard, we find
a mounted trooper holding a led horse, who brings the wagonette to a
stand. The artillery is practising in the Quadrilateral, it appears; passage
along the Route Ronde formally interdicted for the moment. There is
nothing for it but to draw up at the glaring cross-roads and get down to
make fun with the notorious Cocardon, the most ungainly and ill-bred
dog of all the ungainly and ill-bred dogs of Barbizon, or clamber about
the sandy banks. And meanwhile the doctor, with sun umbrella, wide
Panama, and patriarchal beard, is busy wheedling and (for aught the
rest of us know) bribing the too facile sentry. His speech is smooth and
dulcet, his manner dignified and insinuating. It is not for nothing that
the Doctor has voyaged all the world over, and speaks all languages
from French to Patagonian. He has not come borne from perilous journeys to be thwarted by a corporal of horse. And so we soon see the
soldier's mouth relax, and his shoulders imitate a relenting heart. 'En
voiture, Messieurs, Mesdames,' sings the Doctor; and on we go again at
a good round pace, for black care follows hard after us, and discretion
prevails not a little over valour in some timorous spirits of the party. At
any moment we may meet the sergeant, who will send us back. At any
moment we may encounter a flying shell, which will send us somewhere
farther off than Grez.

Grez—for that is our destination—has been highly recommended
for its beauty. 'Il y a de l'eau,' people have said, with an emphasis, as if
that settled the question, which, for a French mind, I am rather led to
think it does. And Grez, when we get there, is indeed a place worthy
of some praise. It lies out of the forest, a cluster of houses, with an old
bridge, an old castle in ruin, and a quaint old church. The inn garden
descends in terraces to the river; stable-yard, kailyard, orchard, and a
space of lawn, fringed with rushes and embellished with a green arbour. On the opposite bank there is a reach of English-looking plain,
set thickly with willows and poplars. And between the two lies the
river, clear and deep, and full of reeds and floating lilies. Water-plants
cluster about the starlings of the long low bridge, and stand half-way
up upon the piers in green luxuriance. They catch the dipped oar with
long antennae, and chequer the slimy bottom with the shadow of their
leaves. And the river wanders and thither hither among the islets, and is
smothered and broken up by the reeds, like an old building in the lithe,
hardy arms of the climbing ivy. You may watch the box where the good
man of the inn keeps fish alive for his kitchen, one oily ripple following
another over the top of the yellow deal. And you can hear a splashing

and a prattle of voices from the shed under the old kirk, where the village women wash and wash all day among the fish and water-lilies. It seems as if linen washed there should be specially cool and sweet.

We have come here for the river. And no sooner have we all bathed than we board the two shallops and push off gaily, and go gliding under the trees and gathering a great treasure of water-lilies. Some one sings; some trail their hands in the cool water; some lean over the gunwale to see the image of the tall poplars far below, and the shadow of the boat, with the balanced oars and their own head protruded, glide smoothly over the yellow floor of the stream. At last, the day declining—all silent and happy, and up to the knees in the wet lilies—we punt slowly back again to the landing-place beside the bridge. There is a wish for solitude on all. One hides himself in the arbour with a cigarette; another goes a walk in the country with Cocardon; a third inspects the church. And it is not till dinner is on the table, and the inn's best wine goes round from glass to glass, that we begin to throw off the restraint and fuse once more into a jolly fellowship.

Half the party are to return to-night with the wagonette; and some of the others, loath to break up company, will go with them a bit of the way and drink a stirrup-cup at Marlotte. It is dark in the wagonette, and not so merry as it might have been. The coachman loses the road. So-and-so tries to light fireworks with the most indifferent success. Some sing, but the rest are too weary to applaud; and it seems as if the festival were fairly at an end—

> 'Nous avons fait la noce,
> Rentrons à nos foyers!'

And such is the burthen, even after we have come to Marlotte and taken our places in the court at Mother Antonine's. There is punch on the long table out in the open air, where the guests dine in summer weather. The candles flare in the night wind, and the faces round the punch are lit up, with shifting emphasis, against a background of complete and solid darkness. It is all picturesque enough; but the fact is, we are aweary. We yawn; we are out of the vein; we have made the wedding, as the song says, and now, for pleasure's sake, let's make an end on't. When here comes striding into the court, booted to mid-thigh, spurred and splashed, in a jacket of green cord, the great, famous, and redoubtable Blank; and in a moment the fire kindles again, and the night is witness of our laughter as he imitates Spaniards, Germans, Englishmen, picture-dealers, all eccentric ways of speaking and thinking, with a possession, a fury, a strain of mind and voice, that would rather suggest a nervous crisis than a desire to please. We are as merry as ever when the trap sets forth again, and say farewell noisily to all the good folk going farther. Then, as we are far enough from thoughts of sleep, we visit Blank in his quaint house, and sit an hour or so in a great tapestried chamber, laid with furs, littered with sleeping hounds, and lit up, in fantastic shadow and shine, by a wood fire in a mediaeval chimney. And then we plod back through the darkness to the inn beside the river.

How quick bright things come to confusion! When we arise next morning, the grey showers fall steadily, the trees hang limp, and the face of the stream is spoiled with dimpling raindrops. Yesterday's lilies encumber the garden walk, or begin, dismally enough, their voyage towards the Seine and the salt sea. A sickly shimmer lies upon the dripping house-roofs, and all the colour is washed out of the green and golden landscape of last night, as though an envious man had taken a water-colour sketch and blotted it together with a sponge. We go out a-walking in the wet roads. But the roads about Grez have a trick of their own. They go on for a while among clumps of willows and patches of vine, and then, suddenly and without any warning, cease and determine in some miry hollow or upon some bald knowe; and you have a short period of hope, then right-about face, and back the way you came! So we draw about the kitchen fire and play a round game of cards for ha'pence, or go to the billiard-room, for a match at corks and by one consent a messenger is sent over for the wagonette—Grez shall be left to-morrow.

To-morrow dawns so fair that two of the party agree to walk back for exercise, and let their kidnap-sacks follow by the trap. I need hardly say they are neither of them French; for, of all English phrases, the phrase 'for exercise' is the least comprehensible across the Straits of Dover. All goes well for a while with the pedestrians. The wet woods are full of scents in the noontide. At a certain cross, where there is a guardhouse, they make a halt, for the forester's wife is the daughter of their good host at Barbizon. And so there they are hospitably received by the comely woman, with one child in her arms and another prattling and tottering at her gown, and drink some syrup of quince in the back parlour, with a map of the forest on the wall, and some prints of love-affairs and the great Napoleon hunting. As they draw near the Quadrilateral, and hear once more the report of the big guns, they take a by-road to avoid the sentries, and go on a while somewhat vaguely, with the sound of the cannon in their ears and the rain beginning to fall. The ways grow wider and sandier; here and there there are real sand-hills, as though by the sea-shore; the fir-wood is open and grows in clumps upon the hillocks, and the race of sign-posts is no more. One begins to look at the other doubtfully. 'I am sure we should keep more to the right,' says one; and the other is just as certain they should hold to the left. And now, suddenly, the heavens open, and the rain falls 'sheer and strong and loud,' as out of a shower-bath. In a moment they are as wet as shipwrecked sailors. They cannot see out of their eyes for the drift, and the water churns and gurgles in their boots. They leave the track and try across country with a gambler's desperatin, for it seems as if it were impossible to make the situation worse; and, for the next hour, go scrambling from boulder to boulder, or plod along paths that are now no more than rivulets, and across waste clearings where the scattered shells and broken fir-trees tell all too plainly of the cannon in the distance. And meantime the cannon grumble out responses to the grumbling thunder. There is such a mixture of melodrama and sheer discomfort about all this, it is at once so grey and so lurid, that it is far more agreeable to read and write about by the chimney-corner than to suffer in the person. At last they chance on the right path, and make Franchard in the early evening, the sorriest pair of wanderers that ever welcomed English ale. Thence, by the Bois d'Hyver, the Ventes-Alexandre, and the Pins Brulés, to the clean hostelry, dry clothes, and dinner.

The Woods in Spring

I think you will like the forest best in the sharp early springtime, when it is just beginning to reawaken, and innumerable violets peep from among the fallen leaves; when two or three people at most sit down to dinner, and, at table, you will do well to keep a rug about your knees, for the nights are chill, and the salle-à-manger opens on the court. There is less to distract the attention, for one thing, and the forest is more itself. It is not bedotted with artists' sunshades as with unknown mushrooms, nor bestrewn with the remains of English picnics. The hunting still goes on, and at any moment your heart may be brought into your mouth as you hear far-away horns; or you may be told by an agitated peasant that the Vicomte has gone up the avenue, not ten minutes since, 'à fond de train, monsieur, et avec douze pipuers.'

If you go up to some coign of vantage in the system of low hills that permeates the forest, you will see many different tracts of country, each of its own cold and melancholy neutral tint, and all mixed together and mingled the one into the other at the seams. You will see tracts of leafless beeches of a faint yellowish grey, and leafless oaks a little ruddier in the hue. Then zones of pine of a solemn green; and, dotted among the pines, or standing by themselves in rocky clearings, the delicate, snow-white trunks of birches, spreading out into snow-white branches yet more delicate, and crowned and canopied with a purple haze of twigs. And then a long, bare ridge of tumbled boulders, with bright sand-breaks between them, and wavering sandy roads among the bracken and brown heather. It is all rather cold and unhomely. It has not the perfect beauty, nor the gem-like colouring, of the wood in the later year, when it is no more than one vast colonnade of verdant shadow, tremulous with insects, intersected here and there by lanes of sunlight set in purple heather. The loveliness of the woods in March is not, assuredly, of this blowzy rustic type. It is made sharp with a grain of salt, with a touch of ugliness. It has a sting like the sting of bitter ale; you acquire the love of it as men acquire a taste for olives. And the wonderful clear, pure air wells into your lungs the while by voluptuous inhalations, and makes the eyes bright, and sets the heart tinkling to a new tune—or, rather, to an old tune; for you remember in your boyhood something akin to this spirit of adventure, this thirst for exploration, that now takes you masterfully by the hand, plunges you into many a deep grove, and drags you over many a stony crest. it is as if the whole wood were full of friendly voice, calling you farther in, and you turn from one side to another, like Buridan's donkey, in a maze of pleasure.

Comely beeches send up their white, straight, clustered branches, barred with green moss, like so many fingers from a half-clenched hand. Mighty oaks stand to the ankles in a fine tracery of underwood; thence the tall shaft climbs upwards, and the great forest of stalwart boughs spreads out into the golden evening sky, where the rooks are flying and calling. On the sward of the Bois d'Hyver the firs stand well asunder with outspread arms, like fencers saluting; and the air smells of resin all around, and the sound of the axe is rarely still. But strangest of all, and in appearance oldest of all, are the dim and wizard upland districts of young wood. The ground is carpeted with fir-tassel, and strewn with fir-apples and flakes of fallen bark. Rocks lie crouching in the thicket, guttered with rain, tufted with lichen, white with years and the rigours of the changeful seasons. Brown and yellow butterflies are sown and carried away again by the light air—like thistledown. The loneliness of these coverts is so excessive, that there are moments when pleasure draws to the verge of fear. You listen and listen for some noise to break the silence, till you grow half mesmerised by the intensity of the strain; your sense of your own identity is troubled; your brain reels, like that of some gymnosophist poring on his own nose in Asiatic jungles; and should you see your own outspread feet, you see them, not as anything of yours, but as a feature of the scene around you.

Still the forest is always, but the stillness is not always unbroken. You can hear the wind pass in the distance over the tree-tops; sometimes briefly, like the noise of a train; sometimes with a long steady rush, like the breaking of waves. And sometimes, close at band, the branches move, a moan goes through the thicket, and the wood thrills to its heart. Perhaps you may hear a carriage on the road to Fontainebleau, a bird gives a dry continual chirp, the dead leaves rustle underfoot, or you may time your steps to the steady recurrent strokes of the woodman's axe. From time to time, over the low grounds, a flight of rooks goes by; and from time to time the cooing of wild doves falls upon the ear, not sweet and rich and near at hand as in England, but a sort of voice of the woods, thin and far away, as fits these solemn places. Or you hear suddenly the hollow, eager, violent barking of dogs; scared deer flit past you through the fringes of the wood; then a man or two running, in green blouse, with gun and game-bag on a bandoleer; and then, out of the thick of the trees, comes the jar of rifle-shots. Or perhaps the hounds are out, and horns are blown, and scarlet-coated huntsmen flash through the clearings, and the solid noise of horses galloping passes below you, where you sit perched among the rocks and heather. The boar is afoot, and all over the forest, and in all neighbouring villages, there is a vague excitement and a vague hope; for who knows whither the chase may lead? and even to have seen a single piqueur, or spoken to a single sportsman, is to be a man of consequence for the night.

Besides men who shoot and men who ride with the hounds, there are few people in the forest, in the early spring, save woodcutters plying their axes steadily, and old women and children gathering wood for the fire. You may meet such a party coming home in the twilight: the old woman laden with a fagot of chips, and the little ones hauling a long branch behind them in her wake. That is the worst of what there is to encounter; and if I tell you of what once happened to a friend of mine, it is by no means to tantalise you with false hopes; for the adventure was unique. It was on a very cold, still, sunless morning, with a flat grey sky and a frosty tingle in the air, that this friend (who shall here be nameless) heard the notes of a key-bugle played with much hesitation, and saw the smoke of a fire spread out along the green pine-tops, in a remote uncanny glen, hard by a hill of naked boulders. He drew near warily, and beheld a picnic party seated under a tree in an open. The old father knitted a sock, the mother sat staring at the fire. The eldest son, in the uniform of a private of dragoons, was choosing out notes on a key-bugle. Two or three daughters lay in the neighbourhood picking violets. And the whole party as grave and silent as the woods around them! My friend watched for a long time, he says; but all held their peace; not one spoke or smiled; only the dragoon kept choosing out single notes upon the bugle, and the father knitted away at his work and made strange movements the while with his flexible eyebrows. They took no notice whatever of my friend's presence, which was disquieting in itself, and increased the resemblance of the whole party to mechanical waxworks. Certainly, he affirms, a wax figure might have played the bugle with more spirit than that strange dragoon. And as this hypothesis of his became more certain, the awful insolubility of why they should be left out there in the woods with nobody to wind them up again when they ran down, and a growing disquietude as to what might happen next, became too much for his courage, and he turned tail, and fairly took to his heels. It might have been a singing in his ears, but he fancies he was followed as he ran by a peal of Titanic laughter. Nothing has ever transpired to clear up the mystery; it may be they were automata; or it may be (and this is the theory to which I lean myself) that this is all another chapter of Heine's 'Gods in Exile'; that the upright old man with the eyebrows was no other than Father Jove, and the young dragoon with the taste for music either Apollo or Mars.

Morality

Strange indeed is the attraction of the forest for the minds of men. Not one or two only, but a great chorus of grateful voices have arisen to spread abroad its fame. Half the famous writers of modern France have had their word to say about Fontainebleau. Chateaubriand, Michelet, Béranger, George Sand, de Senancour, Flaubert, Murger, the brothers Goncourt, Théodore de Banville, each of these has done something to the eternal praise and memory of these woods. Even at the very worst of times, even when the picturesque was anathema in the eyes of all Persons of Taste, the forest still preserved a certain reputation for beauty. It was in 1730 that the Abbé Guilbert published his Historical Description of the Palace, Town, and Forest of Fontainebleau. And very droll it is to see him, as he tries to set forth his admiration in terms of what was then permissible. The monstrous rocks, etc., says the Abbé 'sont admirées avec surprise des voyageurs qui s'écrient aussitôt avec Horace: Ut mihi devio rupee et vacuum nemus mirari libet.' The good man is not exactly lyrical in his praise; and you see how he sets his back against Horace as against a trusty oak. Horace, at any rate, was classical. For the rest, however, the Abbé likes places where many alleys meet; or which, like the Belle-Étoile, are kept up 'by a special gardener,' and admires at the Table du Roi the labours of the Grand Master of Woods and Waters, the Sieur de la Falure, 'qui a fait faire ce magnifique endroit.'

But indeed, it is not so much for its beauty that the forest makes a claim upon men's hearts, as for that subtle something, that quality of the air, that emanation from the old trees, that so wonderfully changes and renews a weary spirit. Disappointed men, sick Francis Firsts and vanquished Grand Monarchs, time out of mind have come here for consolation. Hither perplexed folk have retired out of the press of life, as into a deep bay-window on some night of masquerade, and here found quiet and silence, and rest, the mother of wisdom. It is the great moral spa; this forest without a fountain is itself the great fountain of Juventius. It is the best place in the world to bring an old sorrow that has been a long while your friend and enemy; and if, like Béranger's your gaiety has run away from home and left open the door for sorrow to come in, of all covers in Europe, it is here you may expect to find the truant hid. With every hour you change. The air penetrates through your clothes, and nestles to your living body. You love exercise and slumber, long fasting and full meals. You forget all your scruples and live a while in peace and freedom, and for the moment only. For here, all is absent that can stimulate to moral feeling. Such people as you see may be old, or toil-worn, or sorry; but you see them framed in the forest, like figures on a painted canvas; and for you, they are not people in any living and kindly sense. You forget the grim contrariety of interests. You forget the narrow lane where all men jostle together in unchivalrous contention, and the kennel, deep and unclean, that gapes on either hand for the defeated. Life is simple enough, it seems, and the very idea of sacrifice becomes like a mad fancy out of a last night's dream.

Your ideal is not perhaps high, but it is plain and possible. You become enamoured of a life of change and movement and the open air, where the muscles shall be more exercised than the affections. When you have had your will of the forest, you may visit the whole round world.

You may buckle on your knapsack and take the road on foot. You may bestride a good nag, and ride forth, with a pair of saddle-bags, into the enchanted East. You may cross the Black Forest, and see Germany wide-spread before you, like a map, dotted with old cities, walled and spired, that dream all day on their own reflections in the Rhine or Danube. You may pass the spinal cord of Europe and go down from Alpine glaciers to where Italy extends her marble moles and glasses her marble palaces in the midland sea. You may sleep in flying trains or wayside taverns. You may be awakened at dawn by the scream of the express or the small pipe of the robin in the hedge. For you the rain should allay the dust of the beaten road; the wind dry your clothes upon you as you walked. Autumn should hang out russet pears and purple grapes along the lane; inn after inn proffer you their cups of raw wine; river by river receive your body in the sultry noon. Wherever you went warm valleys and high trees and pleasant villages should compass you about; and light fellowships should take you by the arm, and walk with you an hour upon your way. You may see from afar off what it will come to in the end—the weather-beaten red-nosed vagabond, consumed by a fever of the feet, cut off from all near touch of human sympathy, a waif, an Ishmael, and an outcast. And yet it will seem well—and yet, in the air of the forest, this will seem the best—to break all the network bound about your feet by birth and old companionship and loyal love, and bear your shovelful of phosphates to and fro, in town country, until the hour of the great dissolvent.

Or, perhaps, you will keep to the cover. For the forest is by itself, and forest life owns small kinship with life in the dismal land of labour. Men are so far sophisticated that they cannot take the world as it is given to them by the sight of their eyes. Not only what they see and hear, but what they know to be behind, enter into their notion of a place. If the sea, for instance, lie just across the hills, sea-thoughts will come to them at intervals, and the tenor of their dreams from time to time will suffer a sea-change. And so here, in this forest, a knowledge of its greatness is for much in the effect produced. You reckon up the miles that lie be-tween you and intrusion. You may walk before you all day long, and not fear to touch the barrier of your Eden, or stumble out of fairyland into the land of gin and steam-hammers. And there is an old tale enhances for the imagination the grandeur of the woods of France, and secures you in the thought of your seclusion. When Charles VI. hunted in the time of his wild boyhood near Senlis, there was captured an old stag, having a collar of bronze about his neck, and these words engraved on the collar: 'Caesar mihi hoc donavit.' It is no wonder if the minds of men were moved at this occurrence and they stood aghast to find themselves thus touching hands with forgotten ages, and following an antiquity with hound and horn. And even for you, it is scarcely in an idle curiosity that you ponder how many centuries this stag had carried its free antlers through the wood, and how many summers and winters had shone and snowed on the imperial badge. If the extent of solemn wood could thus safeguard a tall stag from the hunter's hounds and houses, might not you also play hide-and-seek, in these groves, with all the pangs and trepidations of man's life, and elude Death, the mighty hunter, for more than the span of human years? Here, also, crash his arrows; here, in the farthest glade, sounds the gallop of the pale horse. But he does not hunt this cover with all his hounds, for the game is thin and small: and if you were but alert and wary, if you lodged ever in the deepest thickets, you too might live on into later generations and astonish men by your stalwart age and the trophies of an immemorial success.

For the forest takes away from you all excuse to die. There is nothing here to cabin or thwart your free desires. Here all the impudencies of the brawling world reach you no more. You may count your hours, like Endymion, by the strokes of the lone woodcutter, or by the progression of the lights and shadows and the sun wheeling his wide circuit through the naked heavens. Here shall you see no enemies but winter and rough weather. And if a pang comes to you at all, it will be a pang of healthful hunger. All the puling sorrows, all the carking repentance, all this talk of duty that is no duty, in the great peace, in the pure daylight of these woods, fall away from you like a garment. And if perchance you come forth upon an eminence, where the wind blows upon you large and fresh, and the pines knock their long stems together, like an ungainly sort of puppets, and see far away over the plain a factory chimney defined against the pale horizon—it is for you, as for the staid and simple peasant when, with his plough, he upturns old arms and harness from the furrow of the glebe. Ay, sure enough, there was a battle there in the old times; and, sure enough, there is a world out yonder where men strive together with a noise of oaths and weeping and clamorous dispute. So much you apprehend by an athletic act of the imagination. A faint far-off rumour as of Merovingian wars; a legend as of some dead religion.

CHAPTER VI—A MOUNTAIN TOWN IN FRANCE[5] A FRAGMENT 1879

Originally intended to serve as the opening chapter of 'Travels with a Donkey in the Cevennes.'

Le Monastier is the chief place of a hilly canton in Haute Loire, the ancient Velay. As the name betokens, the town is of monastic origin; and it still contains a towered bulk of monastery and a church of some architectural pretensions, the seat of an arch-priest and several vicars. It stands on the side of hill above the river Gazeille, about fifteen miles from Le Puy, up a steep road where the wolves sometime pursue the diligence in winter. The road, which is bound for Vivarais, passes through the town from end to end in a single narrow street; there you may see the fountain where women fill their pitchers; there also some old houses with carved doors and pediment and ornamental work in iron. For Monastier, like Maybole in Ayrshire, was a sort of country capital, where the local aristocracy had their town mansions for the winter; and there is a certain baron still alive and, I am told, extremely penitent, who found means to ruin himself by high living in this village on the hills. He certainly has claims to be considered the most remarkable spendthrift on record. How he set about it, in a place where there are no luxuries for sale, and where the board at the best inn comes to little more than a shilling a day, is a problem for the wise. His son, ruined as the family was, went as far as Paris to sow his wild oats; and so the cases of father and son mark an epoch in the history of centralisation in France. Not until the latter had got into the train was the work of Richelieu complete.

It is a people of lace-makers. The women sit in the streets by groups of five or six; and the noise of the bobbins is audible from one group to another. Now and then you will hear one woman clattering off prayers

---

5   Reprinted by permission of John Lane.

for the edification of the others at their work. They wear gaudy shawls, white caps with a gay ribbon about the head, and sometimes a black felt brigand hat above the cap; and so they give the street colour and brightness and a foreign air. A while ago, when England largely supplied herself from this district with the lace called torchon, it was not unusual to earn five francs a day; and five francs in Monastier is worth a pound in London. Now, from a change in the market, it takes a clever and industrious work-woman to earn from three to four in the week, or less than an eighth of what she made easily a few years ago. The tide of prosperity came and went, as with our northern pitmen, and left nobody the richer. The women bravely squandered their gains, kept the men in idleness, and gave themselves up, as I was told, to sweethearting and a merry life. From week's end to week's end it was one continuous gala in Monastier; people spent the day in the wine-shops, and the drum or the bagpipes led on the bourrées up to ten at night. Now these dancing days are over. 'Il n'y a plus de jeunesse,' said Victor the garçon. I hear of no great advance in what are thought the essentials of morality; but the bourrée, with its rambling, sweet, interminable music, and alert and rustic figures, has fallen into disuse, and is mostly remembered as a custom of the past. Only on the occasion of the fair shall you hear a drum discreetly in a wine-shop or perhaps one of the company singing the measure while the others dance. I am sorry at the change, and marvel once more at the complicated scheme of things upon this earth, and how a turn of fashion in England can silence so much mountain merriment in France. The lace-makers themselves have not entirely forgiven our country-women; and I think they take a special pleasure in the legend of the northern quarter of the town, called L'Anglade, because there the English free-lances were arrested and driven back by the potency of a little Virgin Mary on the wall.

From time to time a market is held, and the town has a season of revival; cattle and pigs are stabled in the streets; and pickpockets have been known to come all the way from Lyons for the occasion. Every Sunday the country folk throng in with daylight to buy apples, to attend mass, and to visit one of the wine-shops, of which there are no fewer than fifty in this little town. Sunday wear for the men is a green tailcoat of some coarse sort of drugget, and usually a complete suit to match. I have never set eyes on such degrading raiment. Here it clings, there bulges; and the human body, with its agreeable and lively lines, is turned into a mockery and laughing-stock. Another piece of Sunday business with the peasants is to take their ailments to the chemist for advice. It is as much a matter for Sunday as church-going. I have seen a woman who had been unable to speak since the Monday before, wheezing, catching her breath, endlessly and painfully coughing; and yet she had waited upwards of a hundred hours before coming to seek help, and had the week been twice as long, she would have waited still. There was a canonical day for consultation; such was the ancestral habit, to which a respectable lady must study to conform.

Two conveyances go daily to Le Puy, but they rival each other in polite concessions rather than in speed. Each will wait an hour or two hours cheerfully while an old lady does her marketing or a gentleman finishes the papers in a café. The Courrier (such is the name of one) should leave Le Puy by two in the afternoon and arrive at Monastier in good on the return voyage, and arrive at Monastier in good time for a six-o'clock dinner. But the driver dares not disoblige his customers. He will postpone his departure again and again, hour after hour; and I have known the sun to go down on his delay. These purely personal favours, this consideration of men's fancies, rather than the hands of a mechanical clock, as marking the advance of the abstraction, time, makes a more humorous business of stage-coaching than we are used to see it.

As far as the eye can reach, one swelling line of hill top rises and falls behind another; and if you climb an eminence, it is only to see new and father ranges behind these. Many little rivers run from all sides in cliffy valleys; and one of them, a few miles from Monastier, bears the great name of Loire. The mean level of the country is a little more than three thousand feet above the sea, which makes the atmosphere proportionally brisk and wholesome. There is little timber except pines, and the greater part of the country lies in moorland pasture. The country is wild and tumbled rather than commanding; an upland rather than a mountain district; and the most striking as well as the most agreeable scenery lies low beside the rivers. There, indeed, you will find many corners that take the fancy; such as made the English noble choose his grave by a Swiss streamlet, where nature is at her freshest, and looks as young as on the seventh morning. Such a place is the course of the Gazeille, where it waters the common of Monastier and thence downwards till it joins the Loire; a place to hear birds singing; a place for lovers to frequent. The name of the river was perhaps suggested by the sound of its passage over the stones; for it is a great warbler, and at night, after I was in bed at Monastier, I could hear it go singing down the valley till I fell asleep.

On the whole, this is a Scottish landscape, although not so noble as the best in Scotland; and by an odd coincidence, the population is, in its way, as Scottish as the country. They have abrupt, uncouth, Fifeshire manners, and accost you, as if you were trespassing, an 'Ou'st-ce que vous allez?' only translatable into the Lowland 'Whaur ye gaun?' They keep the Scottish Sabbath. There is no labour done on that day but to drive in and out the various pigs and sheep and cattle that make so pleasant a tinkling in the meadows. The lace-makers have disappeared from the street. Not to attend mass would involve social degradation; and you may find people reading Sunday books, in particular a sort of Catholic Monthly Visitor on the doings of Our Lady of Lourdes. I remember one Sunday, when I was walking in the country, that I fell on a hamlet and found all the inhabitants, from the patriarch to the baby, gathered in the shadow of a gable at prayer. One strapping lass stood with her back to the wall and did the solo part, the rest chiming in devoutly. Not far off, a lad lay flat on his face asleep among some straw, to represent the worldly element.

Again, this people is eager to proselytise; and the postmaster's daughter used to argue with me by the half-hour about my heresy, until she grew quite flushed. I have heard the reverse process going on between a Scotswoman and a French girl; and the arguments in the two cases were identical. Each apostle based her claim on the superior virtue and attainments of her clergy, and clenched the business with a threat of hell-fire. 'Pas bong pretres ici,' said the Presbyterian, 'bong pretres en Ecosse.' And the postmaster's daughter, taking up the same weapon, plied me, so to speak, with the butt of it instead of the bayonet. We are a hopeful race, it seems, and easily persuaded for our good. One cheerful circumstance I note in these guerilla missions, that each side relies on hell, and Protestant and Catholic alike address themselves to a supposed misgiving in their adversary's heart. And I call it cheerful, for faith is a more supporting quality than imagination.

Here, as in Scotland, many peasant families boast a son in holy orders. And here also, the young men have a tendency to emigrate. It is certainly not poverty that drives them to the great cities or across the seas, for many peasant families, I was told, have a fortune of at least 40,000 francs. The lads go forth pricked with the spirit of adventure and the desire to rise in life, and leave their homespun elders grumbling and wondering over the event. Once, at a village called Laussonne, I met one of these disappointed parents: a drake who had fathered a wild swan and seen it take wing and disappear. The wild swan in question was now an apothecary in Brazil. He had flown by way of Bordeaux, and first landed in America, bareheaded and barefoot, and with a single halfpenny in his pocket. And now he was an apothecary! Such a wonderful thing is an adventurous life! I thought he might as well have stayed at home; but you never can tell wherein a man's life consists, nor in what he sets his pleasure: one to drink, another to marry, a third to write scurrilous articles and be repeatedly caned in public, and now this fourth, perhaps, to be an apothecary in Brazil. As for his old father, he could conceive no reason for the lad's behaviour. 'I had always bread for him,' he said; 'he ran away to annoy me. He loved to annoy me. He had no gratitude.' But at heart he was swelling with pride over his travelled offspring, and he produced a letter out of his pocket, where, as he said, it was rotting, a mere lump of paper rags, and waved it gloriously in the air. 'This comes from America,' he cried, 'six thousand leagues away!' And the wine-shop audience looked upon it with a certain thrill.

I soon became a popular figure, and was known for miles in the country. Ou'st que vous allez? was changed for me into Quoi, vous rentrez au Monastier and in the town itself every urchin seemed to know my name, although no living creature could pronounce it. There was one particular group of lace-makers who brought out a chair for me whenever I went by, and detained me from my walk to gossip. They were filled with curiosity about England, its language, its religion, the dress of the women, and were never weary of seeing the Queen's head on English postage-stamps, or seeking for French words in English Journals. The language, in particular, filled them with surprise.

'Do they speak patois in England?' I was once asked; and when I told them not, 'Ah, then, French?' said they.

'No, no,' I said, 'not French.'

'Then,' they concluded, 'they speak patois.'

You must obviously either speak French or patios. Talk of the force of logic—here it was in all its weakness. I gave up the point, but proceeding to give illustrations of my native jargon, I was met with a new mortification. Of all patios they declared that mine was the most preposterous and the most jocose in sound. At each new word there was a new explosion of laughter, and some of the younger ones were glad to rise from their chairs and stamp about the street in ecstasy; and I looked on upon their mirth in a faint and slightly disagreeable bewilderment. 'Bread,' which sounds a commonplace, plain-sailing monosyllable in England, was the word that most delighted these good ladies of Monastier; it seemed to them frolicsome and racy, like a page of Pickwick;

and they all got it carefully by heart, as a stand-by, I presume, for winter evenings. I have tried it since then with every sort of accent and inflection, but I seem to lack the sense of humour.

They were of all ages: children at their first web of lace, a stripling girl with a bashful but encouraging play of eyes, solid married women, and grandmothers, some on the top of their age and some falling towards decrepitude. One and all were pleasant and natural, ready to laugh and ready with a certain quiet solemnity when that was called for by the subject of our talk. Life, since the fall in wages, had begun to appear to them with a more serious air. The stripling girl would sometimes laugh at me in a provocative and not unadmiring manner, if I judge aright; and one of the grandmothers, who was my great friend of the party, gave me many a sharp word of judgment on my sketches, my heresy, or even my arguments, and gave them with a wry mouth and a humorous twinkle in her eye that were eminently Scottish. But the rest used me with a certain reverence, as something come from afar and not entirely human. Nothing would put them at their ease but the irresistible gaiety of my native tongue. Between the old lady and myself I think there was a real attachment. She was never weary of sitting to me for her portrait, in her best cap and brigand hat, and with all her wrinkles tidily composed, and though she never failed to repudiate the result, she would always insist upon another trial. It was as good as a play to see her sitting in judgment over the last. 'No, no,' she would say, 'that is not it. I am old, to be sure, but I am better-looking than that. We must try again.' When I was about to leave she bade me good-bye for this life in a somewhat touching manner. We should not meet again, she said; it was a long farewell, and she was sorry. But life is so full of crooks, old lady, that who knows? I have said good-bye to people for greater distances and times, and, please God, I mean to see them yet again.

One thing was notable about these women, from the youngest to the oldest, and with hardly an exception. In spite of their piety, they could twang off an oath with Sir Toby Belch in person. There was nothing so high or so low, in heaven or earth or in the human body, but a woman of this neighbourhood would whip out the name of it, fair and square, by way of conversational adornment. My landlady, who was pretty and young, dressed like a lady and avoided patois like a weakness, commonly addressed her child in the language of a drunken bully. And of all the swearers that I ever heard, commend me to an old lady in Gondet, a village of the Loire. I was making a sketch, and her curse was not yet ended when I had finished it and took my departure. It is true she had a right to be angry; for here was her son, a hulking fellow, visibly the worse for drink before the day was well begun. But it was strange to hear her unwearying flow of oaths and obscenities, endless like a river, and now and then rising to a passionate shrillness, in the clear and silent air of the morning. In city slums, the thing might have passed unnoticed; but in a country valley, and from a plain and honest countrywoman, this beastliness of speech surprised the ear.

The Conductor, as he is called, of Roads and Bridges was my principal companion. He was generally intelligent, and could have spoken more or less falsetto on any of the trite topics; but it was his specially to have a generous taste in eating. This was what was most indigenous in the man; it was here he was an artist; and I found in his company what I had long suspected, that enthusiasm and special knowledge are the great social qualities, and what they are about, whether white sauce or Shakespeare's plays, an altogether secondary question.

I used to accompany the Conductor on his professional rounds, and grew to believe myself an expert in the business. I thought I could make an entry in a stone-breaker's time-book, or order manure off the wayside with any living engineer in France. Gondet was one of the places we visited together; and Laussonne, where I met the apothecary's father, was another. There, at Laussonne, George Sand spent a day while she was gathering materials for the Marquis de Villemer; and I have spoken with an old man, who was then a child running about the inn kitchen, and who still remembers her with a sort of reverence. It appears that he spoke French imperfectly; for this reason George Sand chose him for companion, and whenever he let slip a broad and picturesque phrase in patois, she would make him repeat it again and again till it was graven in her memory. The word for a frog particularly pleased her fancy; and it would be curious to know if she afterwards employed it in her works. The peasants, who knew nothing of betters and had never so much as heard of local colour, could not explain her chattering with this backward child; and to them she seemed a very homely lady and far from beautiful: the most famous man-killer of the age appealed so little to Velaisian swine-herds!

On my first engineering excursion, which lay up by Crouzials towards Mount Mezenc and the borders of Ardèche, I began an improving acquaintance with the foreman road-mender. He was in great glee at having me with him, passed me off among his subalterns as the supervising engineer, and insisted on what he called 'the gallantry' of paying for my breakfast in a roadside wine-shop. On the whole, he was a man of great weather-wisdom, some spirits, and a social temper. But I am afraid he was superstitious. When he was nine years old, he had seen one night a company of bourgeois et dames qui faisaient la manège avec des chaises, and concluded that he was in the presence of a witches' Sabbath. I suppose, but venture with timidity on the suggestion, that this may have been a romantic and nocturnal picnic party. Again, coming from Pradelles with his brother, they saw a great empty cart drawn by six enormous horses before them on the road. The driver cried aloud and filled the mountains with the cracking of his whip. He never seemed to go faster than a walk, yet it was impossible to overtake him; and at length, at the corner of a hill, the whole equipage disappeared bodily into the night. At the time, people said it was the devil qui s'amusait à faire ca.

I suggested there was nothing more likely, as he must have some amusement.

The foreman said it was odd, but there was less of that sort of thing than formerly. 'C'est difficile,' he added, 'à expliquer.'

When we were well up on the moors and the Conductor was trying some road-metal with the gauge—

'Hark!' said the foreman, 'do you hear nothing?'

We listened, and the wind, which was blowing chilly out of the east, brought a faint, tangled jangling to our ears.

'It is the flocks of Vivarais,' said he.

For every summer, the flocks out of all Ardèche are brought up to pasture on these grassy plateaux.

Here and there a little private flock was being tended by a girl, one spinning with a distaff, another seated on a wall and intently making lace. This last, when we addressed her, leaped up in a panic and put out her arms, like a person swimming, to keep us at a distance, and it was some seconds before we could persuade her of the honesty of our intentions.

The Conductor told me of another herdswoman from whom he had once asked his road while he was yet new to the country, and who fled from him, driving her beasts before her, until he had given up the information in despair. A tale of old lawlessness may yet be read in these uncouth timidities.

The winter in these uplands is a dangerous and melancholy time. Houses are snowed up, and way-farers lost in a flurry within hail of their own fireside. No man ventures abroad without meat and a bottle of wine, which he replenishes at every wine-shop; and even thus equipped he takes the road with terror. All day the family sits about the fire in a foul and airless hovel, and equally without work or diversion. The father may carve a rude piece of furniture, but that is all that will be done until the spring sets in again, and along with it the labours of the field. It is not for nothing that you find a clock in the meanest of these mountain habitations. A clock and an almanac, you would fancy, were indispensable in such a life . . .

CHAPTER VII—RANDOM MEMORIES:
ROSA QUO LOCORUM

Through what little channels, by what hints and premonitions, the consciousness of the man's art dawns first upon the child, it should be not only interesting but instructive to inquire. A matter of curiosity to-day, it will become the ground of science to-morrow. From the mind of childhood there is more history and more philosophy to be fished up than from all the printed volumes in a library. The child is conscious of an interest, not in literature but in life. A taste for the precise, the adroit, or the comely in the use of words, comes late; but long before that he has enjoyed in books a delightful dress rehearsal of experience. He is first conscious of this material—I had almost said this practical—pre-occupation; it does not follow that it really came the first. I have some old fogged negatives in my collection that would seem to imply a prior stage 'The Lord is gone up with a shout, and God with the sound of a trumpet'—memorial version, I know not where to find the text—rings still in my ear from my first childhood, and perhaps with something of my nurses accent. There was possibly some sort of image written in my mind by these loud words, but I believe the words themselves were what I cherished. I had about the same time, and under the same influence—that of my dear nurse—a favourite author: it is possible the reader has not heard of him—the Rev. Robert Murray M'Cheyne. My nurse and I admired his name exceedingly, so that I must have been taught the love of beautiful sounds before I was breeched; and I remember two specimens of his muse until this day:—

'Behind the hills of Naphtali
The sun went slowly down,

> *Leaving on mountain, tower, and tree,*
> *A tinge of golden brown.'*

There is imagery here, and I set it on one side. The other—it is but a verse—not only contains no image, but is quite unintelligible even to my comparatively instructed mind, and I know not even how to spell the outlandish vocable that charmed me in my childhood:

> *'Jehovah Tschidkenu is nothing to her';*[6]—

I may say, without flippancy, that he was nothing to me either, since I had no ray of a guess of what he was about; yet the verse, from then to now, a longer interval than the life of a generation, has continued to haunt me.

I have said that I should set a passage distinguished by obvious and pleasing imagery, however faint; for the child thinks much in images, words are very live to him, phrases that imply a picture eloquent beyond their value. Rummaging in the dusty pigeon-holes of memory, I came once upon a graphic version of the famous Psalm, 'The Lord is my shepherd': and from the places employed in its illustration, which are all in the immediate neighbourhood of a house then occupied by my father, I am able, to date it before the seventh year of my age, although it was probably earlier in fact. The 'pastures green' were represented by a certain suburban stubble-field, where I had once walked with my nurse, under an autumnal sunset, on the banks of the Water of Leith: the place is long ago built up; no pastures now, no stubble-fields; only a maze of little streets and smoking chimneys and shrill children. Here, in the fleecy person of a sheep, I seemed to myself to follow something unseen, unrealised, and yet benignant; and close by the sheep in which I was incarnated—as if for greater security—rustled the skirt, of my nurse. 'Death's dark vale' was a certain archway in the Warriston Cemetery: a formidable yet beloved spot, for children love to be afraid,—in measure as they love all experience of vitality. Here I beheld myself some paces ahead (seeing myself, I mean, from behind) utterly alone in that uncanny passage; on the one side of me a rude, knobby, shepherd's staff, such as cheers the heart of the cockney tourist, on the other a rod like a billiard cue, appeared to accompany my progress; the stiff sturdily upright, the billiard cue inclined confidentially, like one whispering, towards my ear. I was aware—I will never tell you how—that the presence of these articles afforded me encouragement. The third and last of my pictures illustrated words:—

---

6   'Jehovah Tsidkenu,' translated in the Authorised Version as 'The Lord our Righteousness' (Jeremiah xxiii. 6 and xxxiii. 16).

'My table Thou hast furnished
In presence of my foes:
My head Thou dost with oil anoint,
And my cup overflows':

and this was perhaps the most interesting of the series. I saw myself seated in a kind of open stone summer-house at table; over my shoulder a hairy, bearded, and robed presence anointed me from an authentic shoe-horn; the summer-house was part of the green court of a ruin, and from the far side of the court black and white imps discharged against me ineffectual arrows. The picture appears arbitrary, but I can trace every detail to its source, as Mr. Brock analysed the dream of Alan Armadale. The summer-house and court were muddled together out of Billings' Antiquities of Scotland; the imps conveyed from Bagster's Pilgrim's Progress; the bearded and robed figure from any one of the thousand Bible pictures; and the shoe-horn was plagiarised from an old illustrated Bible, where it figured in the hand of Samuel anointing Saul, and had been pointed out to me as a jest by my father. It was shown me for a jest, remark; but the serious spirit of infancy adopted it in earnest. Children are all classics; a bottle would have seemed an intermediary too trivial—that divine refreshment of whose meaning I had no guess; and I seized on the idea of that mystic shoe-horn with delight, even as, a little later, I should have written flagon, chalice, hanaper, beaker, or any word that might have appealed to me at the moment as least contaminate with mean associations. In this string of pictures I believe the gist of the psalm to have consisted; I believe it had no more to say to me; and the result was consolatory. I would go to sleep dwelling with restfulness upon these images; they passed before me, besides, to an appropriate music; for I had already singled out from that rude psalm the one lovely verse which dwells in the minds of all, not growing old, not disgraced by its association with long Sunday tasks, a scarce conscious joy in childhood, in age a companion thought:—

'In pastures green Thou leadest me,
The quiet waters by.'

The remainder of my childish recollections are all of the matter of what was read to me, and not of any manner in the words. If these pleased me it was unconsciously; I listened for news of the great vacant world upon whose edge I stood; I listened for delightful plots that I might re-enact in play, and romantic scenes and circumstances that I might call up before me, with closed eyes, when I was tired of Scotland,

and home, and that weary prison of the sick-chamber in which I lay so long in durance. Robinson Crusoe; some of the books of that cheerful, ingenious, romantic soul, Mayne Reid; and a work rather gruesome and bloody for a child, but very picturesque, called Paul Blake; these are the three strongest impressions I remember: The Swiss Family Robinson came next, longo intervallo. At these I played, conjured up their scenes, and delighted to hear them rehearsed unto seventy times seven. I am not sure but what Paul Blake came after I could read. It seems connected with a visit to the country, and an experience unforgettable. The day had been warm; H—and I had played together charmingly all day in a sandy wilderness across the road; then came the evening with a great flash of colour and a heavenly sweetness in the air. Somehow my play-mate had vanished, or is out of the story, as the sages say, but I was sent into the village on an errand; and, taking a book of fairy tales, went down alone through a fir-wood, reading as I walked. How often since then has it befallen me to be happy even so; but that was the first time: the shock of that pleasure I have never since forgot, and if my mind serves me to the last, I never shall, for it was then that I knew I loved reading.

II

To pass from hearing literature to reading it is to take a great and dangerous step. With not a few, I think a large proportion of their pleasure then comes to an end; 'the malady of not marking' overtakes them; they read thenceforward by the eye alone and hear never again the chime of fair words or the march of the stately period. Non ragioniam of these. But to all the step is dangerous; it involves coming of age; it is even a kind of second weaning. In the past all was at the choice of others; they chose, they digested, they read aloud for us and sang to their own tune the books of childhood. In the future we are to approach the silent, inexpressive type alone, like pioneers; and the choice of what we are to read is in our own hands thenceforward. For instance, in the passages already adduced, I detect and applaud the ear of my old nurse; they were of her choice, and she imposed them on my infancy, reading the works of others as a poet would scarce dare to read his own; gloating on the rhythm, dwelling with delight on assonances and alliterations. I know very well my mother must have been all the while trying to educate my taste upon more secular authors; but the vigour and the continual opportunities of my nurse triumphed, and after a long search, I can find in these earliest volumes of my autobiography no mention of anything but nursery rhymes, the Bible, and Mr. M'Cheyne.

I suppose all children agree in looking back with delight on their school Readers. We might not now find so much pathos in 'Bingen on the Rhine,' 'A soldier of the Legion lay dying in Algiers,' or in 'The Soldier's Funeral,' in the declamation of which I was held to have surpassed myself. 'Robert's voice,' said the master on this memorable occasion, 'is not strong, but impressive': an opinion which I was fool enough to carry home to my father; who roasted me for years in consequence. I am sure one should not be so deliciously tickled by the humorous pieces:—

> *'What, crusty? cries Will in a taking,*
> *Who would not be crusty with half a year's baking?'*

I think this quip would leave us cold. The 'Isles of Greece' seem rather tawdry too; but on the 'Address to the Ocean,' or on 'The Dying Gladiator,' 'time has writ no wrinkle.'

> *'Tis the morn, but dim and dark,*
> *Whither flies the silent lark?'*—

does the reader recall the moment when his eye first fell upon these lines in the Fourth Reader; and 'surprised with joy, impatient as the wind,' he plunged into the sequel? And there was another piece, this time in prose, which none can have forgotten; many like me must have searched Dickens with zeal to find it again, and in its proper context, and have perhaps been conscious of some inconsiderable measure of disappointment, that it was only Tom Pinch who drove, in such a pomp of poetry, to London.

But in the Reader we are still under guides. What a boy turns out for himself, as he rummages the bookshelves, is the real test and pleasure. My father's library was a spot of some austerity; the proceedings of learned societies, some Latin divinity, cyclopaedias, physical science, and, above all, optics, held the chief place upon the shelves, and it was only in holes and corners that anything really legible existed as by accident. The Parent's Assistant, Rob Roy, Waverley, and Guy Mannering, the Voyages of Captain Woods Rogers, Fuller's and Bunyan's Holy Wars, The Reflections of Robinson Crusoe, The Female Bluebeard, G. Sand's Mare au Diable—(how came it in that grave assembly!), Ainsworth's Tower of London, and four old volumes of Punch—these were the chief exceptions. In these latter, which made for years the chief of my diet, I very early fell in love (almost as soon as I could spell) with the Snob Papers. I knew them almost by heart, particularly the visit to the Pontos; and I remember my surprise when I found, long afterwards, that they were famous, and signed with a famous name; to me, as I read and admired them, they were the works of Mr. Punch. Time and again I tried to read Rob Roy, with whom of course I was acquainted from the Tales of a Grandfather; time and again the early part, with Rashleigh and (think of it!) the adorable Diana, choked me off; and I shall never forget the pleasure and surprise with which, lying on the floor one summer evening, I struck of a sudden into the first scene with Andrew Fairservice. 'The worthy Dr. Lightfoot'—'mistrysted with a bogle'—'a wheen green trash'—'Jenny, lass, I think I ha'e her': from that day to this the phrases have been unforgotten. I read on, I need scarce say; I came to Glasgow, I bided tryst on Glasgow Bridge, I met Rob Roy and the Bailie in the Tolbooth, all with transporting pleasure; and then the clouds gathered once more about my path; and I dozed and skipped until I stumbled half-asleep into the clachan of Aberfoyle, and the voices of Iverach and Galbraith recalled me to myself. With that scene and the defeat of Captain Thornton the book concluded; Helen and her sons shocked even the little schoolboy of nine or ten with their unreality; I read no more, or I did not grasp what I was read-ing; and years elapsed before I consciously met Diana and her father among the hills, or saw Rashleigh dying in the chair. When I think of that novel and that evening, I am impatient with all others; they seem but shadows and impostors; they cannot satisfy the appetite which this awakened; and I dare be known to think it the best of Sir Walter's by nearly as much as Sir Walter is the best of novelists. Perhaps Mr. Lang is right, and our first friends in the land of fiction are always the most real. And yet I had read before this Guy Mannering, and some of Waverley, with no such delighted sense of truth and humour, and I read immediately after the greater part of the Waverley Novels, and was never moved again in the same way or to the same degree. One circumstance is suspicious: my critical estimate of the Waverley Novels has scarce changed at all since I was ten. Rob Roy, Guy Mannering, and Redgauntlet first; then, a little lower; The Fortunes of Nigel; then, after a huge gulf, Ivanhoe and Anne of Geierstein: the rest nowhere; such was the verdict of the boy. Since then The Antiquary, St. Ronan's Well, Kenilworth, and The Heart of Midlothian have gone up in the scale; perhaps Ivanhoe and Anne of Geierstein have gone a trifle down; Diana Vernon has been added to my admirations in that enchanted world of Rob Roy; I think more of the letters in Redgauntlet, and Peter Peebles, that dreadful piece of realism, I can now read about with equanimity, interest, and I had almost said pleasure, while to the childish critic he often caused unmixed distress. But the rest is the same; I could not finish The Pirate when I was a child, I have never finished it yet; Peveril of the Peak dropped half way through from my schoolboy hands, and though I have since waded to an end in a kind of wager with myself, the exercise was quite without enjoyment. There is something disquieting in these considerations. I still think the visit to Ponto's the best part of the Book of Snobs: does that mean that I was right when I was a child, or does it mean that I have never grown since then, that the child is not the man's father, but the man? and that I came into the world with all my faculties complete, and have only learned sinsyne to be more tolerant of boredom? . . .

CHAPTER VIII—THE IDEAL HOUSE

Two things are necessary in any neighbourhood where we propose to spend a life: a desert and some living water.

There are many parts of the earth's face which offer the necessary combination of a certain wildness with a kindly variety. A great prospect is desirable, but the want may be otherwise supplied; even greatness can be found on the small scale; for the mind and the eye measure differently. Bold rocks near hand are more inspiriting than distant Alps, and the thick fern upon a Surrey heath makes a fine forest for the imagination, and the dotted yew trees noble mountains. A Scottish moor with birches and firs grouped here and there upon a knoll, or one of those rocky seaside deserts of Provence overgrown with rosemary and thyme and smoking with aroma, are places where the mind is never weary. Forests, being more enclosed, are not at first sight so attractive, but they exercise a spell; they must, however, be diversified with either heath or rock, and are hardly to be considered perfect without conifers. Even sand-hills, with their intricate plan, and their gulls and rabbits, will stand well for the necessary desert.

The house must be within hail of either a little river or the sea. A great river is more fit for poetry than to adorn a neighbourhood; its sweep of waters increases the scale of the scenery and the distance of one notable object from another; and a lively burn gives us, in the space of a few yards, a greater variety of promontory and islet, of cascade, shallow goil, and boiling pool, with answerable changes both of song and colour, than a navigable stream in many hundred miles. The fish, too, make a more considerable feature of the brookside, and the trout plumping in the shadow takes the ear. A stream should, besides, be narrow enough to cross, or the burn hard by a bridge, or we are at once shut out of Eden. The quantity of water need be of no concern, for the mind sets the scale, and can enjoy a Niagara Fall of thirty inches. Let us approve the singer of

> *'Shallow rivers, by whose falls*
> *Melodious birds sing madrigals.'*

If the sea is to be our ornamental water, choose an open seaboard with a heavy beat of surf; one much broken in outline, with small havens and dwarf headlands; if possible a few islets; and as a first necessity, rocks reaching out into deep water. Such a rock on a calm day is a better station than the top of Teneriffe or Chimborazo. In short, both for the desert and the water, the conjunction of many near and bold details is bold scenery for the imagination and keeps the mind alive.

Given these two prime luxuries, the nature of the country where we are to live is, I had almost said, indifferent; after that inside the garden, we can construct a country of our own. Several old trees, a considerable variety of level, several well-grown hedges to divide our garden into provinces, a good extent of old well-set turf, and thickets of shrubs and ever-greens to be cut into and cleared at the new owner's pleasure, are the qualities to be sought for in your chosen land. Nothing is more delightful than a succession of small lawns, opening one out of the other through tall hedges; these have all the charm of the old bowling-green repeated, do not require the labour of many trimmers, and afford a series of changes. You must have much lawn against the early summer, so as to have a great field of daisies, the year's morning frost; as you must have a wood of lilacs, to enjoy to the full the period of their blossoming. Hawthorn is another of the Spring's ingredients; but it is even best to have a rough public lane at one side of your enclosure which, at the right season, shall become an avenue of bloom and odour. The old flowers are the best and should grow carelessly in corners. Indeed, the ideal fortune is to find an old garden, once very richly cared for, since sunk into neglect, and to tend, not repair, that neglect; it will thus have a smack of nature and wildness which skilful dispositions cannot overtake. The gardener should be an idler, and have a gross partiality to the kitchen plots: an eager or toilful gardener misbecomes the garden landscape; a tasteful gardener will be ever meddling, will keep the borders raw, and take the bloom off nature. Close adjoining, if you are in the south, an olive-yard, if in the north, a swarded apple-orchard reaching to the stream, completes your miniature domain; but this is perhaps best entered through a door in the high fruit-wall; so that you close the door behind you on your sunny plots, your hedges and evergreen jungle, when you go down to watch the apples falling in the pool. It is a golden maxim to cultivate the garden for the nose, and the eyes will take care of themselves. Nor must the ear be forgotten: without birds a garden is a prison-yard. There is a garden near Marseilles on a steep hill-side, walking by which, upon a sunny morning, your ear will suddenly be ravished with a burst of small and very cheerful singing: some score of cages being set out there to sun their occupants. This is a heavenly surprise to any passer-by; but the price paid, to keep so many ardent and winged creatures from their liberty, will make the luxury too dear for any thoughtful pleasure-lover. There is only one sort of bird that I can tolerate caged, though even then I think it hard, and that is what is called in France the Bec-d'Argent. I once had two of these pigmies in captivity; and in the quiet, hire house upon a silent street where I was then living, their song, which was not much louder than a bee's, but airily musical, kept me in a perpetual good humour. I put the cage upon my table when I worked, carried it with me when I went for meals, and kept it by my head at night: the first thing in the morning, these maestrini would pipe up. But these, even if you can pardon their imprisonment, are for the house. In the garden the wild birds must plant a colony, a chorus of the lesser warblers that should be almost deafening, a blackbird in the lilacs, a nightingale down the lane, so that you must stroll to hear it, and yet a little farther, tree-tops populous with rooks.

Your house should not command much outlook; it should be set deep and green, though upon rising ground, or, if possible, crowning a knoll, for the sake of drainage. Yet it must be open to the east, or you will miss the sunrise; sunset occurring so much later, you can go up a few steps and look the other way. A house of more than two stories is a mere barrack; indeed the ideal is of one story, raised upon cellars. If the rooms are large, the house may be small: a single room, lofty, spacious, and lightsome, is more palatial than a castleful of cabinets and cup-boards. Yet size in a house, and some extent and intricacy of corridor, is certainly delightful to the flesh. The reception room should be, if possible, a place of many recesses, which are 'petty retiring places for conference'; but it must have one long wall with a divan: for a day spent upon a divan, among a world of cushions, is as full of diversion as to travel. The eating-room, in the French mode, should be ad hoc: unfurnished, but with a buffet, the table, necessary chairs, one or two of Canaletto's etchings, and a tile fire-place for the winter. In neither of these public places should there be anything beyond a shelf or two of books; but the passages may be one library from end to end, and the stair, if there be one, lined with volumes in old leather, very brightly carpeted, and leading half-way up, and by way of landing, to a windowed recess with a fire-place; this window, almost alone in the house, should command a handsome prospect. Husband and wife must each possess a studio; on the woman's sanctuary I hesitate to dwell, and turn to the man's. The walls are shelved waist-high for books, and the top thus forms a continuous table running round the wall. Above are prints, a large map of the neighbourhood, a Corot and a Claude or two. The room is very spacious, and the five tables and two chairs are but as islands. One table is for actual work, one close by for references in use; one, very large, for MSS. or proofs that wait their turn; one kept clear for an occasion; and the fifth is the map table, groaning under a collection of large-scale maps and charts. Of all books these are the least wearisome to read and the richest in matter; the course of roads and rivers, the contour lines and the forests in the maps—the reefs, soundings, anchors, sailing marks and little pilot-pictures in the charts—and, in both, the bead-roll of names, make them of all printed matter the most fit to stimulate and satisfy the fancy. The chair in which you write is very low and easy, and backed into a corner; at one elbow the fire twinkles; close at the other, if you are a little inhumane, your cage of silver-bills are twittering into song.

Joined along by a passage, you may reach the great, sunny, glass-roofed, and tiled gymnasium, at the far end of which, lined with bright marble, is your plunge and swimming bath, fitted with a capacious boiler.

The whole loft of the house from end to end makes one undivided chamber; here are set forth tables on which to model imaginary or actual countries in putty or plaster, with tools and hardy pigments; a carpenter's bench; and a spared corner for photography, while at the far end a space is kept clear for playing soldiers. Two boxes contain the two armies of some five hundred horse and foot; two others the ammunition of each side, and a fifth the foot-rules and the three colours of chalk, with which you lay down, or, after a day's play, refresh the outlines of the country; red or white for the two kinds of road (according as they are suitable or not for the passage of ordnance), and blue for the course of the obstructing rivers. Here I foresee that you may pass much happy time; against a good adversary a game may well continue for a month; for with armies so considerable three moves will occupy an hour. It will be found to set an excellent edge on this diversion if one of the players shall, every day or so, write a report of the operations in the character of army correspondent.

I have left to the last the little room for winter evenings. This should be furnished in warm positive colours, and sofas and floor thick with rich furs. The hearth, where you burn wood of aromatic quality on silver dogs, tiled round about with Bible pictures; the seats deep and easy; a single Titian in a gold frame; a white bust or so upon a bracket; a rack for the journals of the week; a table for the books of the year; and close in a corner the three shelves full of eternal books that never weary: Shakespeare, Molière, Montaigne, Lamb, Sterne, De Musset's comedies (the one volume open at Carmosine and the other at Fantasio); the Arabian Nights, and kindred stories, in Weber's solemn volumes; Borrow's Bible in Spain, the Pilgrim's Progress, Guy Mannering and Rob Roy, Monte Cristo and the Vicomte de Bragelonne, immortal Boswell sole among biographers, Chaucer, Herrick, and the State Trials.

The bedrooms are large, airy, with almost no furniture, floors of varnished wood, and at the bed-head, in case of insomnia, one shelf of books of a particular and dippable order, such as Pepys, the Paston Letters, Burt's Letters from the Highlands, or the Newgate Calendar. . . .

CHAPTER IX—DAVOS IN WINTER

A mountain valley has, at the best, a certain prison-like effect on the imagination, but a mountain valley, an Alpine winter, and an invalid's weakness make up among them a prison of the most effective kind. The roads indeed are cleared, and at least one footpath dodging up the hill; but to these the health-seeker is rigidly confined. There are for him no cross-cuts over the field, no following of streams, no unguided rambles in the wood. His walks are cut and dry. In five or six different directions he can push as far, and no farther, than his strength permits; never deviating from the line laid down for him and beholding at each repetition the same field of wood and snow from the same corner of the road. This, of itself, would be a little trying to the patience in the course of months; but to this is added, by the heaped mantle of the snow, an almost utter absence of detail and an almost unbroken identity of colour. Snow, it is true, is not merely white. The sun touches it with roseate and golden lights. Its own crushed infinity of crystals, its own richness of tiny sculpture, fills it, when regarded near at hand, with wonderful depths of coloured shadow, and, though wintrily transformed, it is still water, and has watery tones of blue. But, when all is said, these fields of white and blots of crude black forest are but a trite and staring substitute for the infinite variety and pleasantness of the earth's face. Even a boulder, whose front is too precipitous to have retained the snow, seems, if you come upon it in your walk, a perfect gem of colour, reminds you almost painfully of other places, and brings into your head the delights of more Arcadian days—the path across the meadow, the hazel dell, the lilies on the stream, and the scents, the colours, and the whisper of the woods. And scents here are as rare as colours. Unless you get a gust of kitchen in passing some hotel, you shall smell nothing all day long but the faint and choking odour of frost. Sounds, too, are absent: not a bird pipes, not a bough waves, in the dead, windless atmosphere. If a sleigh goes by, the sleigh-bells ring, and that is all; you work all winter through to no other accompaniment but the crunching of your steps upon the frozen snow.

It is the curse of the Alpine valleys to be each one village from one end to the other. Go where you please, houses will still be in sight, before and behind you, and to the right and left. Climb as high as an invalid is able, and it is only to spy new habitations nested in the wood. Nor is that all; for about the health resort the walks are besieged by single people walking rapidly with plaids about their shoulders, by sudden troops of German boys trying to learn to jodel, and by German couples silently and, as you venture to fancy, not quite happily, pursuing love's young dream. You may perhaps be an invalid who likes to make bad verses as he walks about. Alas! no muse will suffer this imminence of interruption—and at the second stampede of jodellers you find your modest inspiration fled. Or you may only have a taste for solitude; it may try your nerves to have some one always in front whom you are visibly overtaking, and some one always behind who is audibly overtaking you, to say nothing of a score or so who brush past you in an opposite direction. It may annoy you to take your walks and seats in public view. Alas! there is no help for it among the Alps. There are no recesses, as in Gorbio Valley by the oil-mill; no sacred solitude of olive gardens on the Roccabruna-road; no nook upon Saint Martin's Cape, haunted by the voice of breakers, and fragrant with the threefold sweetness of the rosemary and the sea-pines and the sea.

For this publicity there is no cure, and no alleviation; but the storms of which you will complain so bitterly while they endure, chequer and by their contrast brighten the sameness of the fair-weather scenes. When sun and storm contend together—when the thick clouds are broken up and pierced by arrows of golden daylight—there will be startling rearrangements and transfigurations of the mountain summits. A sun-dazzling spire of alp hangs suspended in mid-sky among awful glooms and blackness; or perhaps the edge of some great mountain shoulder will be designed in living gold, and appear for the duration of a glance bright like a constellation, and alone 'in the unapparent.' You may think you know the figure of these hills; but when they are thus revealed, they belong no longer to the things of earth—meteors we should rather call them, appearances of sun and air that endure but for a moment and return no more. Other variations are more lasting, as when, for instance, heavy and wet snow has fallen through some windless hours, and the thin, spiry, mountain pine trees stand each stock-still and loaded with a shining burthen. You may drive through a forest so disguised, the tongue-tied torrent struggling silently in the cleft of the ravine, and all still except the jingle of the sleigh bells, and you shall fancy yourself in some untrodden northern territory—Lapland, Labrador, or Alaska.

Or, possibly, you arise very early in the morning; totter down stairs in a state of somnambulism; take the simulacrum of a meal by the glimmer of one lamp in the deserted coffee-room; and find yourself by seven o'clock outside in a belated moonlight and a freezing chill. The mail sleigh takes you up and carries you on, and you reach the top of the ascent in the first hour of the day. To trace the fires of the sunrise as they pass from peak to peak, to see the unlit tree-tops stand out soberly against the lighted sky, to be for twenty minutes in a wonderland of clear, fading shadows, disappearing vapours, solemn blooms of dawn, hills half glorified already with the day and still half confounded with the greyness of the western heaven—these will seem to repay you for the discomforts of that early start; but as the hour proceeds, and these enchantments vanish, you will find yourself upon the farther side in yet another Alpine valley, snow white and coal black, with such another long-drawn congeries of hamlets and such another senseless watercourse bickering along the foot. You have had your moment; but you have not changed the scene. The mountains are about you like a trap; you cannot foot it up a hillside and behold the sea as a great plain, but live in holes and corners, and can change only one for another.

CHAPTER X—HEALTH AND MOUNTAINS

There has come a change in medical opinion, and a change has followed in the lives of sick folk. A year or two ago and the wounded soldiery of mankind were all shut up together in some basking angle of the Riviera, walking a dusty promenade or sitting in dusty olive-yards within earshot of the interminable and unchanging surf—idle among spiritless idlers; not perhaps dying, yet hardly living either, and aspiring, sometimes fiercely, after livelier weather and some vivifying change. These were certainly beautiful places to live in, and the climate was wooing in its softness. Yet there was a later shiver in the sunshine; you were not certain whether you were being wooed; and these mild shores would sometimes seem to you to be the shores of death. There was a lack of a manly element; the air was not reactive; you might write bits of poetry and practise resignation, but you did not feel that here was a good spot to repair your tissue or regain your nerve. And it appears, after all, that there was something just in these appreciations. The invalid is now asked to lodge on wintry Alps; a ruder air shall medicine him; the demon of cold is no longer to be fled from, but bearded in his den. For even Winter has his 'dear domestic cave,' and in those places where he may be said to dwell for ever tempers his austerities.

Any one who has travelled westward by the great transcontinental railroad of America must remember the joy with which he perceived, after the tedious prairies of Nebraska and across the vast and dismal moorlands of Wyoming, a few snowy mountain summits alone, the southern sky. It is among these mountains in the new State of Colorado that the sick man may find, not merely an alleviation of his ailments, but the possibility of an active life and an honest livelihood. There, no longer as a lounger in a plaid, but as a working farmer, sweating at his work, he may prolong and begin anew his life. Instead of the bath-chair, the spade; instead of the regulated walk, rough journeys in the forest, and the pure, rare air of the open mountains for the miasma of the sick-room—these are the changes offered him, with what promise of pleasure and of self-respect, with what a revolution in all his hopes and terrors, none but an invalid can know. Resignation, the cowardice that apes a kind of courage and that lives in the very air of health resorts, is cast aside at a breath of such a prospect. The man can open the door; he can be up and doing; he can be a kind of a man after all and not merely an invalid.

But it is a far cry to the Rocky Mountains. We cannot all of us go farming in Colorado; and there is yet a middle term, which combines the medical benefits of the new system with the moral drawbacks of the old. Again the invalid has to lie aside from life and its wholesome duties; again he has to be an idler among idlers; but this time at a great altitude, far among the mountains, with the snow piled before his door and the frost flowers every morning on his window. The mere fact is tonic to his nerves. His choice of a place of wintering has somehow to his own eyes the air of an act of bold contract; and, since he has wilfully sought low temperatures, he is not so apt to shudder at a touch of chill. He came for that, he looked for it, and he throws it from him with the thought.

A long straight reach of valley, wall-like mountains upon either hand that rise higher and higher and shoot up new summits the higher you climb; a few noble peaks seen even from the valley; a village of hotels; a world of black and white—black pine-woods, clinging to the sides of the valley, and white snow flouring it, and papering it between the pine-woods, and covering all the mountains with a dazzling curd; add a few score invalids marching to and fro upon the snowy road, or skating on the ice-rinks, possibly to music, or sitting under sunshades by the door of the hotel—and you have the larger features of a mountain sanatorium. A certain furious river runs curving down the valley; its pace never varies, it has not a pool for as far as you can follow it; and its unchanging, senseless hurry is strangely tedious to witness. It is a river that a man could grow to hate. Day after day breaks with the rarest gold upon the mountain spires, and creeps, growing and glowing, down into the valley. From end to end the snow reverberates the sunshine; from end to end the air tingles with the light, clear and dry like crystal. Only along the course of the river, but high above it, there hangs far into the noon, one waving scarf of vapour. It were hard to fancy a more engaging feature in a landscape; perhaps it is harder to believe that delicate, long-lasting phantom of the atmosphere, a creature of the incontinent stream whose course it follows. By noon the sky is arrayed in an unrivalled pomp of colour—mild and pale and melting in the north, but towards the zenith, dark with an intensity of purple blue. What with this darkness of heaven and the intolerable lustre of the snow, space is reduced again to chaos. An English painter, coming to France late in life, declared with natural anger that 'the values were all wrong.' Had he got among the Alps on a bright day he might have lost his reason. And even to any one who has looked at landscape with any care, and in any way through the spectacles of representative art, the scene has a character of insanity. The distant shining mountain peak is here beside your eye; the neighbouring dull-coloured house in comparison is miles away; the summit, which is all of splendid snow, is close at hand; the nigh slopes, which are black with pine trees, bear it no relation, and might be in another sphere. Here there are none of those delicate gradations, those intimate, misty joinings-on and spreadings-out into the distance, nothing of that art of air and light by which the face of nature explains and veils itself in climes which we may be allowed to think more lovely. A glaring piece of crudity, where everything that is not white is a solecism and defies the judgment of the eyesight; a scene of blinding definition; a parade of daylight, almost scenically vulgar, more than scenically trying, and yet hearty and healthy, making the nerves to tighten and the mouth to smile: such is the winter daytime in the Alps.

With the approach of evening all is changed. A mountain will suddenly intercept the sun; a shadow fall upon the valley; in ten minutes the thermometer will drop as many degrees; the peaks that are no longer shone upon dwindle into ghosts; and meanwhile, overhead, if the weather be rightly characteristic of the place, the sky fades towards night through a surprising key of colours. The latest gold leaps from the last mountain. Soon, perhaps, the moon shall rise, and in her gentler light the valley shall be mellowed and misted, and here and there a wisp of silver cloud upon a hilltop, and here and there a warmly glowing window in a house, between fire and starlight, kind and homely in the fields of snow.

But the valley is not seated so high among the clouds to be eternally exempt from changes. The clouds gather, black as ink; the wind bursts rudely in; day after day the mists drive overhead, the snow-flakes flutter down in blinding disarray; daily the mail comes in later from the top of the pass; people peer through their windows and foresee no end but an entire seclusion from Europe, and death by gradual dry-rot, each in his indifferent inn; and when at last the storm goes, and the sun comes again, behold a world of unpolluted snow, glossy like fur, bright like daylight, a joy to wallowing dogs and cheerful to the souls of men. Or perhaps from across storied and malarious Italy, a wind cunningly winds about the mountains and breaks, warm and unclean, upon our mountain valley. Every nerve is set ajar; the conscience recognises, at a gust, a load of sins and negligences hitherto unknown; and the whole invalid world huddles into its private chambers, and silently recognises the empire of the Fohn.

CHAPTER XI—ALPINE DIVERSIONS

There will be no lack of diversion in an Alpine sanitarium. The place is half English, to be sure, the local sheet appearing in double column, text and translation; but it still remains half German; and hence we have a band which is able to play, and a company of actors able, as you will be told, to act. This last you will take on trust, for the players, unlike the local sheet, confine themselves to German and though at the beginning of winter they come with their wig-boxes to each hotel in turn, long before Christmas they will have given up the English for a bad job. There will follow, perhaps, a skirmish between the two races; the German element seeking, in the interest of their actors, to raise a mysterious item, the Kur-taxe, which figures heavily enough already in the weekly bills, the English element stoutly resisting. Meantime in the English hotels home-played farces, tableaux-vivants, and even balls enliven the evenings; a charity bazaar sheds genial consternation; Christmas and New Year are solemnised with Pantagruelian dinners, and from time to time the young folks carol and revolve untunefully enough through the figures of a singing quadrille.

A magazine club supplies you with everything, from the Quarterly to the Sunday at Home. Grand tournaments are organised at chess, draughts, billiards and whist. Once and again wandering artists drop into our mountain valley, coming you know not whence, going you cannot imagine whither, and belonging to every degree in the hierarchy of musical art, from the recognised performer who announces a concert for the evening, to the comic German family or solitary long-haired German baritone, who surprises the guests at dinner-time with songs and a collection. They are all of them good to see; they, at least, are moving; they bring with them the sentiment of the open road; yesterday, perhaps, they were in Tyrol, and next week they will be far in Lombardy, while all we sick folk still simmer in our mountain prison. Some of them, too, are welcome as the flowers in May for their own sake; some of them may have a human voice; some may have that magic which transforms a wooden box into a song-bird, and what we jeeringly call a fiddle into what we mention with respect as a violin. From that grinding lilt, with which the blind man, seeking pence, accompanies the beat of paddle wheels across the ferry, there is surely a difference rather of kind than of degree to that unearthly voice of singing that bewails and praises the destiny of man at the touch of the true virtuoso. Even that you may perhaps enjoy; and if you do so you will own it impossible to enjoy it more keenly than here, im Schnee der Alpen. A hyacinth in a pot, a handful of primroses packed in moss, or a piece of music by some one who knows the way to the heart of a violin, are things that, in this invariable sameness of the snows and frosty air, surprise you like an adventure. It is droll, moreover, to compare the respect with which the invalids attend a concert, and the ready contempt with which they greet the dinner-time performers. Singing which they would hear with real enthusiasm—possibly with tears—from a corner of a drawing-room, is listened to with laughter when it is offered by an unknown professional and no money has been taken at the door.

Of skating little need be said; in so snowy a climate the rinks must be intelligently managed; their mismanagement will lead to many days of vexation and some petty quarrelling, but when all goes well, it is certainly curious, and perhaps rather unsafe, for the invalid to skate under a burning sun, and walk back to his hotel in a sweat, through long tracts of glare and passages of freezing shadow. But the peculiar outdoor sport of this district is tobogganing. A Scotchman may remember the low flat board, with the front wheels on a pivot, which was called a hurlie; he may remember this contrivance, laden with boys, as, laboriously started, it ran rattling down the brae, and was, now successfully, now unsuccessfully, steered round the corner at the foot; he may remember scented summer evenings passed in this diversion, and many a grazed skin, bloody cockscomb, and neglected lesson. The toboggan is to the hurlie what the sled is to the carriage; it is a hurlie upon runners; and if for a grating road you substitute a long declivity of beaten snow, you can imagine the giddy career of the tobogganist. The correct position is to sit; but the fantastic will sometimes sit hind-foremost, or dare the descent upon their belly or their back. A few steer with a pair of pointed sticks, but it is more classical to use the feet. If the weight be heavy and the track smooth, the toboggan takes the bit between its teeth; and to steer a couple of full-sized friends in safety requires not only judgment but desperate exertion. On a very steep track, with a keen evening frost, you may have moments almost too appalling to be called enjoyment; the head goes, the world vanishes; your blind steed bounds below your weight; you reach the foot, with all the breath knocked out of your body, jarred and bewildered as though you had just been subjected to a railway accident. Another element of joyful horror is added by the formation of a train; one toboggan being tied to another, perhaps to the number of half a dozen, only the first rider being allowed to steer, and all the rest pledged to put up their feet and follow their leader, with heart in mouth, down the mad descent. This, particularly if the track begins with a headlong plunge, is one of the most exhilarating follies in the world, and the tobogganing invalid is early reconciled to somersaults.

There is all manner of variety in the nature of the tracks, some miles in length, others but a few yards, and yet like some short rivers, furious in their brevity. All degrees of skill and courage and taste may be suited in your neighbourhood. But perhaps the true way to toboggan is alone and at night. First comes the tedious climb, dragging your instrument behind you. Next a long breathing-space, alone with snow and pinewoods, cold, silent and solemn to the heart. Then you push of; the toboggan fetches way; she begins to feel the hill, to glide, to, swim, to gallop. In a breath you are out from under the pine trees, and a whole heavenful of stars reels and flashes overhead. Then comes a vicious effort; for by this time your wooden steed is speeding like the wind, and you are spinning round a corner, and the whole glittering valley and all the lights in all the great hotels lie for a moment at your feet; and the next you are racing once more in the shadow of the night with close-shut teeth and beating heart. Yet a little while and you will be landed on the highroad by the door of your own hotel. This, in an atmosphere tingling with forty degrees of frost, in a night made luminous with stars and snow, and girt with strange white mountains, teaches the pulse an unaccustomed tune and adds a new excitement to the life of man upon his planet.

CHAPTER XII—THE STIMULATION OF THE ALPS

To any one who should come from a southern sanitarium to the Alps, the row of sun-burned faces round the table would present the first surprise. He would begin by looking for the invalids, and he would lose his pains, for not one out of five of even the bad cases bears the mark of sickness on his face. The plump sunshine from above and its strong reverberation from below colour the skin like an Indian climate; the treatment, which consists mainly of the open air, exposes even the sickliest to tan, and a tableful of invalids comes, in a month or two, to resemble a tableful of hunters. But although he may be thus surprised at the first glance, his astonishment will grow greater, as he experiences the effects of the climate on himself. In many ways it is a trying business to reside upon the Alps: the stomach is exercised, the appetite often languishes; the liver may at times rebel; and because you have come so far from metropolitan advantages, it does not follow that you shall recover. But one thing is undeniable—that in the rare air, clear, cold, and blinding light of Alpine winters, a man takes a certain troubled delight in his existence which can nowhere else be paralleled. He is perhaps no happier, but he is stingingly alive. It does not, perhaps, come out of him in work or exercise, yet he feels an enthusiasm of the blood unknown in more temperate climates. It may not be health, but it is fun.

There is nothing more difficult to communicate on paper than this baseless ardour, this stimulation of the brain, this sterile joyousness of spirits. You wake every morning, see the gold upon the snow-peaks, become filled with courage, and bless God for your prolonged existence. The valleys are but a stride to you; you cast your shoe over the hilltops; your ears and your heart sing; in the words of an unverified quotation from the Scotch psalms, you feel yourself fit /'on the wings of all the winds' to 'come flying all abroad.' Europe and your mind are too narrow for that flood of energy. Yet it is notable that you are hard to root out of your bed; that you start forth, singing, indeed, on your walk, yet are unusually ready to turn home again; that the best of you is volatile; and that although the restlessness remains till night, the strength is early at an end. With all these heady jollities, you are half conscious of an underlying languor in the body; you prove not to be so well as you had fancied; you weary before you have well begun; and though you mount at morning with the lark, that is not precisely a song-bird's heart that you bring back with you when you return with aching limbs and peevish temper to your inn.

It is hard to say wherein it lies, but this joy of Alpine winters is its own reward. Baseless, in a sense, it is more than worth more permanent improvements. The dream of health is perfect while it lasts; and if, in trying to realise it, you speedily wear out the dear hallucination, still every day, and many times a day, you are conscious of a strength you scarce possess, and a delight in living as merry as it proves to be transient.

The brightness—heaven and earth conspiring to be bright—the levity and quiet of the air; the odd stirring silence—more stirring than a tumult; the snow, the frost, the enchanted landscape: all have their part in the effect and on the memory, 'tous vous tapent sur la téte'; and yet when you have enumerated all, you have gone no nearer to explain or even to qualify the delicate exhilaration that you feel—delicate, you may say, and yet excessive, greater than can be said in prose, almost greater than an invalid can bear. There is a certain wine of France known in England in some gaseous disguise, but when drunk in the land of its nativity still as a pool, clean as river water, and as heady as verse. It is more than probable that in its noble natural condition this was the very wine of Anjou so beloved by Athos in the 'Musketeers.' Now, if the reader has ever washed down a liberal second breakfast with the wine in question, and gone forth, on the back of these dilutions, into a sultry, sparkling noontide, he will have felt an influence almost as genial, although strangely grosser, than this fairy titillation of the nerves among the snow and sunshine of the Alps. That also is a mode, we need not say of intoxication, but of insobriety. Thus also a man walks in a strong sunshine of the mind, and follows smiling, insubstantial meditations. And whether he be really so clever or so strong as he supposes, in either case he will enjoy his chimera while it lasts.

The influence of this giddy air displays itself in many secondary ways. A certain sort of laboured pleasantry has already been recognised, and may perhaps have been remarked in these papers, as a sort peculiar to that climate. People utter their judgments with a cannonade of syllables; a big word is as good as a meal to them; and the turn of a phrase goes further than humour or wisdom. By the professional writer many sad vicissitudes have to be undergone. At first he cannot write at all. The heart, it appears, is unequal to the pressure of business, and the brain, left without nourishment, goes into a mild decline. Next, some power of work returns to him, accompanied by jumping headaches. Last, the spring is opened, and there pours at once from his pen a world of blatant, hustling polysyllables, and talk so high as, in the old joke, to be positively offensive in hot weather. He writes it in good faith and with a sense of inspiration; it is only when he comes to read what he has written that surprise and disquiet seize upon his mind. What is he to do, poor man? All his little fishes talk like whales. This yeasty inflation, this stiff and strutting architecture of the sentence has come upon him while he slept; and it is not he, it is the Alps, who are to blame. He is not, perhaps, alone, which somewhat comforts him. Nor is the ill without a remedy. Some day, when the spring returns, he shall go down a little lower in this world, and remember quieter inflections and more modest language. But here, in the meantime, there seems to swim up some outline of a new cerebral hygiene and a good time coming, when experienced advisers shall send a man to the proper measured level for the ode, the biography, or the religious tract; and a nook may be found between the sea and Chimborazo, where Mr. Swinburne shall be able to write more continently, and Mr. Browning somewhat slower.

Is it a return of youth, or is it a congestion of the brain? It is a sort of congestion, perhaps, that leads the invalid, when all goes well, to face the new day with such a bubbling cheerfulness. It is certainly congestion that makes night hideous with visions, all the chambers of a many-storeyed caravanserai, haunted with vociferous nightmares, and many wakeful people come down late for breakfast in the morning. Upon that theory the cynic may explain the whole affair—exhilaration, nightmares, pomp of tongue and all. But, on the other hand, the peculiar blessedness of boyhood may itself be but a symptom of the same complaint, for the two effects are strangely similar; and the frame of mind of the invalid upon the Alps is a sort of intermittent youth, with periods of lassitude. The fountain of Juventus does not play steadily in these parts; but there it plays, and possibly nowhere else.

CHAPTER XIII—ROADS—1873

No amateur will deny that he can find more pleasure in a single draw-ing, over which he can sit a whole quiet forenoon, and so gradu-ally study himself into humour with the artist, than he can ever extract from the dazzle and accumulation of incongruous impressions that send him, weary and stupefied, out of some famous picture-gallery. But what is thus admitted with regard to art is not extended to the (so-called) natural beauties no amount of excess in sublime mountain outline or the graces of cultivated lowland can do anything, it is supposed, to weaken or degrade the palate. We are not at all sure, however, that modera-tion, and a regimen tolerably austere, even in scenery, are not healthful and strengthening to the taste; and that the best school for a lover of nature is not to the found in one of those countries where there is no stage effect—nothing salient or sudden,—but a quiet spirit of orderly and harmonious beauty pervades all the details, so that we can patiently attend to each of the little touches that strike in us, all of them together, the subdued note of the landscape. It is in scenery such as this that we find ourselves in the right temper to seek out small sequestered love-liness. The constant recurrence of similar combinations of colour and outline gradually forces upon us a sense of how the harmony has been built up, and we become familiar with something of nature's manner-ism. This is the true pleasure of your 'rural voluptuary,'—not to remain awe-stricken before a Mount Chimborazo; not to sit deafened over the big drum in the orchestra, but day by day to teach himself some new beauty—to experience some new vague and tranquil sensation that has before evaded him. It is not the people who 'have pined and hungered after nature many a year, in the great city pent,' as Coleridge said in the poem that made Charles Lamb so much ashamed of himself; it is not those who make the greatest progress in this intimacy with her, or who are most quick to see and have the greatest gusto to enjoy. In this, as in everything else, it is minute knowledge and long-continued loving industry that make the true dilettante. A man must have thought much over scenery before he begins fully to enjoy it. It is no youngling enthusiasm on hilltops that can possess itself of the last essence of beauty. Probably most people's heads are growing bare before they can see all in a landscape that they have the capability of seeing; and, even then, it will be only for one little moment of consummation before the faculties are again on the decline, and they that look out of the windows begin to be darkened and restrained in sight. Thus the study of nature should be carried forward thoroughly and with system. Every gratification should be rolled long under the tongue, and we should be always eager to analyse and compare, in order that we may be able to give some plausible reason for our admirations. True, it is difficult to put even approximately into words the kind of feelings thus called into play. There is a dangerous vice inherent in any such intellectual refining upon vague sensation. The analysis of such satisfactions lends itself very readily to literary affectations; and we can all think of instances where it has shown itself apt to exercise a morbid influence, even upon an author's choice of language and the turn of his sentences. And yet there is much that makes the attempt attractive; for any expression, however imperfect, once given to a cherished feeling, seems a sort of legitimation of the pleasure we take in it. A common sentiment is one of those great goods that make life palatable and ever new. The knowledge that another has felt as we have felt, and seen things, even if they are little things, not much otherwise than we have seen them, will continue to the end to be one of life's choicest pleasures.

Let the reader, then, betake himself in the spirit we have recommended to some of the quieter kinds of English landscape. In those homely and placid agricultural districts, familiarity will bring into relief many things worthy of notice, and urge them pleasantly home to him by a sort of loving repetition; such as the wonderful life-giving speed of windmill sails above the stationary country; the occurrence and recurrence of the same church tower at the end of one long vista after another: and, conspicuous among these sources of quiet pleasure, the character and variety of the road itself, along which he takes his way. Not only near at hand, in the lithe contortions with which it adapts itself to the interchanges of level and slope, but far away also, when he sees a few hundred feet of it upheaved against a hill and shining in the afternoon sun, he will find it an object so changeful and enlivening that he can always pleasurably busy his mind about it. He may leave the river-side, or fall out of the way of villages, but the road he has always with him; and, in the true humour of observation, will find in that sufficient company. From its subtle windings and changes of level there arises a keen and continuous interest, that keeps the attention ever alert and cheerful. Every sensitive adjustment to the contour of the ground, every little dip and swerve, seems instinct with life and an exquisite sense of balance and beauty. The road rolls upon the easy slopes of the country, like a long ship in the hollows of the sea. The very margins of waste ground, as they trench a little farther on the beaten way, or recede again to the shelter of the hedge, have something of the same free delicacy of line—of the same swing and wilfulness. You might think for a whole summer's day (and not have thought it any nearer an end by evening) what concourse and succession of circumstances has produced the least of these deflections; and it is, perhaps, just in this that we should look for the secret of their interest. A foot-path across a meadow—in all its human waywardness and unaccountability, in all the grata protervitas of its varying direction—will always be more to us than a railroad well engineered through a difficult country.[7] No reasoned sequence is thrust upon our attention: we seem to have slipped for one lawless little moment out of the iron rule of cause and effect; and so we revert at once to some of the pleasant old heresies of personification, always poetically orthodox, and attribute a sort of free-will, an active and spontaneous life, to the white riband of road that lengthens out, and bends, and cunningly adapts itself to the inequalities of the land before our eyes. We remember, as we write, some miles of fine wide highway laid out with conscious aesthetic artifice through a broken and richly cultivated tract of country. It is said that the engineer had Hogarth's line of beauty in his mind as he laid them down. And the result is striking. One splendid satisfying sweep passes with easy transition into another, and there is nothing to trouble or dislocate the strong continuousness of the main line of the road. And yet there is something wanting. There is here no saving imperfection, none of those secondary curves and little trepidations of direction that carry, in natural roads, our curiosity actively along with them. One feels at once that this road has not has been laboriously grown like a natural road, but made to pattern; and that, while a model may be academically correct in outline, it will always be inanimate and cold. The traveller is

---

7   Compare Blake, in the *Marriage of Heaven and Hell:* 'Improvement makes straight roads; but the crooked roads, without improvement, are roads of Genius.'

also aware of a sympathy of mood between himself and the road he travels. We have all seen ways that have wandered into heavy sand near the sea-coast, and trail wearily over the dunes like a trodden serpent. Here we too must plod forward at a dull, laborious pace; and so a sympathy is preserved between our frame of mind and the expression of the relaxed, heavy curves of the roadway. Such a phenomenon, indeed, our reason might perhaps resolve with a little trouble. We might reflect that the present road had been developed out of a tract spontaneously followed by generations of primitive wayfarers; and might see in its expression a testimony that those generations had been affected at the same ground, one after another, in the same manner as we are affected to-day. Or we might carry the reflection further, and remind ourselves that where the air is invigorating and the ground firm under the traveller's foot, his eye is quick to take advantage of small undulations, and he will turn carelessly aside from the direct way wherever there is anything beautiful to examine or some promise of a wider view; so that even a bush of wild roses may permanently bias and deform the straight path over the meadow; whereas, where the soil is heavy, one is preoccupied with the labour of mere progression, and goes with a bowed head heavily and unobservantly forward. Reason, however, will not carry us the whole way; for the sentiment often recurs in situations where it is very hard to imagine any possible explanation; and indeed, if we drive briskly along a good, well-made road in an open vehicle, we shall experience this sympathy almost at its fullest. We feel the sharp settle of the springs at some curiously twisted corner; after a steep ascent, the fresh air dances in our faces as we rattle precipitately down the other side, and we find it difficult to avoid attributing something headlong, a sort of *abandon*, to the road itself.

The mere winding of the path is enough to enliven a long day's walk in even a commonplace or dreary country-side. Something that we have seen from miles back, upon an eminence, is so long hid from us, as we wander through folded valleys or among woods, that our expectation of seeing it again is sharpened into a violent appetite, and as we draw nearer we impatiently quicken our steps and turn every corner with a beating heart. It is through these prolongations of expectancy, this succession of one hope to another, that we live out long seasons of pleasure in a few hours' walk. It is in following these capricious sinuosities that we learn, only bit by bit and through one coquettish reticence after another, much as we learn the heart of a friend, the whole loveliness of the country. This disposition always preserves something new to be seen, and takes us, like a careful cicerone, to many different points of distant view before it allows us finally to approach the hoped-for destination.

In its connection with the traffic, and whole friendly intercourse with the country, there is something very pleasant in that succession of saunterers and brisk and business-like passers-by, that peoples our ways and helps to build up what Walt Whitman calls 'the cheerful voice of the public road, the gay, fresh sentiment of the road.' But out of the great network of ways that binds all life together from the hill-farm to the city, there is something individual to most, and, on the whole, nearly as much choice on the score of company as on the score of beauty or easy travel. On some we are never long without the sound of wheels, and folk pass us by so thickly that we lose the sense of their number. But on others, about little-frequented districts, a meeting is an affair of moment; we have the sight far off of some one coming towards us, the growing definiteness of the person, and then the brief passage and salutation, and the road left empty in front of us for perhaps a great while to come. Such encounters have a wistful interest that can hardly be understood by the dweller in places more populous. We remember standing beside a countryman once, in the mouth of a quiet by-street in a city that was more than ordinarily crowded and bustling; he seemed stunned and bewildered by the continual passage of different faces; and after a long pause, during which he appeared to search for some suitable expression, he said timidly that there seemed to be a *great deal of meeting thereabouts.* The phrase is significant. It is the expression of town-life in the language of the long, solitary country highways. A meeting of one with one was what this man had been used to in the pastoral uplands from which he came; and the concourse of the streets was in his eyes only an extraordinary multiplication of such 'meetings.'

And now we come to that last and most subtle quality of all, to that sense of prospect, of outlook, that is brought so powerfully to our minds by a road. In real nature, as well as in old landscapes, beneath that impartial daylight in which a whole variegated plain is plunged and saturated, the line of the road leads the eye forth with the vague sense of desire up to the green limit of the horizon. Travel is brought home to us, and we visit in spirit every grove and hamlet that tempts us in the distance. Sehnsucht—the passion for what is ever beyond—is livingly expressed in that white riband of possible travel that severs the uneven country; not a ploughman following his plough up the shining furrow, not the blue smoke of any cottage in a hollow, but is brought to us with a sense of nearness and attainability by this wavering line of junction. There is a passionate paragraph in Werther that strikes the very key. 'When I came hither,' he writes, 'how the beautiful valley invited me on every side, as I gazed down into it from the hill-top! There the wood—ah, that I might mingle in its shadows! there the mountain summits—ah, that I might look down from them over the broad country! the interlinked hills! the secret valleys! Oh to lose myself among their mysteries! I hurried into the midst, and came back without finding aught I hoped for. Alas! the distance is like the future. A vast whole lies in the twilight before our spirit; sight and feeling alike plunge and lose themselves in the prospect, and we yearn to surrender our whole being, and let it be filled full with all the rapture of one single glorious sensation; and alas! when we hasten to the fruition, when *there* is changed to *here,* all is afterwards as it was before, and we stand in our indigent and cramped estate, and our soul thirsts after a still ebbing elixir.' It is to this wandering and uneasy spirit of anticipation that roads minister. Every little vista, every little glimpse that we have of what lies before us, gives the impatient imagination rein, so that it can outstrip the body and already plunge into the shadow of the woods, and overlook from the hill-top the plain beyond it, and wander in the windings of the valleys that are still far in front. The road is already there—we shall not be long behind. It is as if we were marching with the rear of a great army, and, from far before, heard the acclamation of the people as the vanguard entered some friendly and jubilant city. Would not every man, through all the long miles of march, feel as if he also were within the gates?

CHAPTER XIV—ON THE ENJOYMENT OF UNPLEASANT PLACES—1874

It is a difficult matter to make the most of any given place, and we have much in our own power. Things looked at patiently from one side after another generally end by showing a side that is beautiful. A few months ago some words were said in the Portfolio as to an 'austere regimen in scenery'; and such a discipline was then recommended as 'healthful and strengthening to the taste.' That is the text, so to speak, of the present essay. This discipline in scenery, it must be understood, is something more than a mere walk before breakfast to whet the appetite. For when we are put down in some unsightly neighbourhood, and especially if we have come to be more or less dependent on what we see, we must set ourselves to hunt out beautiful things with all the ardour and patience of a botanist after a rye plant. Day by day we perfect ourselves in the art of seeing nature more favourably. We learn to live with her, as people learn to live with fretful or violent spouses: to dwell lovingly on what is good, and shut our eyes against all that is bleak or inharmonious. We learn, also, to come to each place in the right spirit. The traveller, as Brantôme quaintly tells us, 'fait des discours en soi pour soutenir en chemin'; and into these discourses he weaves something out of all that he sees and suffers by the way; they take their tone greatly from the varying character of the scene; a sharp ascent brings different thoughts from a level road; and the man's fancies grow lighter as he comes out of the wood into a clearing. Nor does the scenery any more affect the thoughts than the thoughts affect the scenery. We see places through our humours as through differently coloured glasses. We are ourselves a term in the equation, a note of the chord, and make discord or harmony almost at will. There is no fear for the result, if we can but surrender ourselves sufficiently to the country that surrounds and follows us, so that we are ever thinking suitable thoughts or telling ourselves some suitable sort of story as we go. We become thus, in some sense, a centre of beauty; we are provocative of beauty, much as a gentle and sincere character is provocative of sincerity and gentleness in others. And even where there is no harmony to be elicited by the quickest and most obedient of spirits, we may still embellish a place with some attraction of romance. We may learn to go far afield for associations, and handle them lightly when we have found them. Sometimes an old print comes to our aid; I have seen many a spot lit up at once with picturesque imaginations, by a reminiscence of Callot, or Sadeler, or Paul Brill. Dick Turpin has been my lay figure for many an English lane. And I suppose the Trossachs would hardly be the Trossachs for most tourists if a man of admirable romantic instinct had not peopled it for them with harmonious figures, and brought them thither with minds rightly prepared for the impression. There is half the battle in this preparation. For instance: I have rarely been able to visit, in the proper spirit, the wild and inhospitable places of our own Highlands. I am happier where it is tame and fertile, and not readily pleased without trees. I understand that there are some phases of mental trouble that harmonise well with such surroundings, and that some persons, by the dispensing power of the imagination, can go back several centuries in spirit, and put themselves into sympathy with the hunted, houseless, unsociable way of life that was in its place upon these savage hills. Now, when I am sad, I like nature to charm me out of my sadness, like David before Saul; and the thought of these past ages strikes nothing in me but an unpleasant pity; so that I can never hit on the right humour for this sort of landscape, and lose much pleasure in consequence. Still, even here, if I were only let alone, and time enough were given, I should have all manner of pleasures, and take many clear and beautiful images away with me when I left. When we cannot think ourselves into sympathy with the great features of a country, we learn to ignore them, and put our head among the grass for flowers, or pore, for long times together, over the changeful current of a stream. We come down to the sermon in stones, when we are shut out from any poem in the spread landscape. We begin to peep and botanise, we take an interest in birds and insects, we find many things beautiful in miniature. The reader will recollect the little summer scene in Wuthering Heights—the one warm scene, perhaps, in all that powerful, miserable novel—and the great feature that is made therein by grasses and flowers and a little sunshine: this is in the spirit of which I now speak. And, lastly, we can go indoors; interiors are sometimes as beautiful, often more picturesque, than the shows of the open air, and they have that quality of shelter of which I shall presently have more to say.

With all this in mind, I have often been tempted to put forth the paradox that any place is good enough to live a life in, while it is only in a few, and those highly favoured, that we can pass a few hours agreeably. For, if we only stay long enough we become at home in the neighbourhood. Reminiscences spring up, like flowers, about uninteresting corners. We forget to some degree the superior loveliness of other places, and fall into a tolerant and sympathetic spirit which is its own reward and justification. Looking back the other day on some recollections of my own, I was astonished to find how much I owed to such a residence; six weeks in one unpleasant country-side had done more, it seemed, to quicken and educate my sensibilities than many years in places that jumped more nearly with my inclination.

The country to which I refer was a level and tree-less plateau, over which the winds cut like a whip. For miles and miles it was the same. A river, indeed, fell into the sea near the town where I resided; but the valley of the river was shallow and bald, for as far up as ever I had the heart to follow it. There were roads, certainly, but roads that had no beauty or interest; for, as there was no timber, and but little irregularity of surface, you saw your whole walk exposed to you from the beginning: there was nothing left to fancy, nothing to expect, nothing to see by the wayside, save here and there an unhomely-looking homestead, and here and there a solitary, spectacled stone-breaker; and you were only accompanied, as you went doggedly forward, by the gaunt telegraph-posts and the hum of the resonant wires in the keen sea-wind. To one who had learned to know their song in warm pleasant places by the Mediterranean, it seemed to taunt the country, and make it still bleaker by suggested contrast. Even the waste places by the side of the road were not, as Hawthorne liked to put it, 'taken back to Nature' by any decent covering of vegetation. Wherever the land had the chance, it seemed to lie fallow. There is a certain tawny nudity of the South, bare sunburnt plains, coloured like a lion, and hills clothed only in the blue transparent air; but this was of another description—this was the nakedness of the North; the earth seemed to know that it was naked, and was ashamed and cold.

It seemed to be always blowing on that coast. Indeed, this had passed into the speech of the inhabitants, and they saluted each other when they met with 'Breezy, breezy,' instead of the customary 'Fine day' of farther south. These continual winds were not like the harvest breeze, that just keeps an equable pressure against your face as you walk, and serves to set all the trees talking over your head, or bring round you the smell of the wet surface of the country after a shower. They were of the bitter, hard, persistent sort, that interferes with sight and respiration, and makes the eyes sore. Even such winds as these have their own merit in proper time and place. It is pleasant to see them brandish great masses of shadow. And what a power they have over the colour of the world! How they ruffle the solid woodlands in their passage, and make them shudder and whiten like a single willow! There is nothing more vertiginous than a wind like this among the woods, with all its sights and noises; and the effect gets between some painters and their sober eyesight, so that, even when the rest of their picture is calm, the foliage is coloured like foliage in a gale. There was nothing, however, of this sort to be noticed in a country where there were no trees and hardly any shadows, save the passive shadows of clouds or those of rigid houses and walls. But the wind was nevertheless an occasion of pleasure; for nowhere could you taste more fully the pleasure of a sudden lull, or a place of opportune shelter. The reader knows what I mean; he must remember how, when he has sat himself down behind a dyke on a hillside, he delighted to hear the wind hiss vainly through the crannies at his back; how his body tingled all over with warmth, and it began to dawn upon him, with a sort of slow surprise, that the country was beautiful, the heather purple, and the far-away hills all marbled with sun and shadow. Wordsworth, in a beautiful passage of the 'Prelude,' has used this as a figure for the feeling struck in us by the quiet by-streets of London after the uproar of the great thoroughfares; and the comparison may be turned the other way with as good effect:—

> 'Meanwhile the roar continues, till at length,
> Escaped as from an enemy, we turn
> Abruptly into some sequester'd nook,
> Still as a shelter'd place when winds blow loud!'

I remember meeting a man once, in a train, who told me of what must have been quite the most perfect instance of this pleasure of escape. He had gone up, one sunny, windy morning, to the top of a great cathedral somewhere abroad; I think it was Cologne Cathedral, the great unfinished marvel by the Rhine; and after a long while in dark stairways, he issued at last into the sunshine, on a platform high above the town. At that elevation it was quite still and warm; the gale was only in the lower strata of the air, and he had forgotten it in the quiet interior of the church and during his long ascent; and so you may judge of his surprise when, resting his arms on the sunlit balustrade and looking over into the Place far below him, he saw the good people holding on their hats and leaning hard against the wind as they walked. There is something, to my fancy, quite perfect in this little experience of my fellow-traveller's. The ways of men seem always very trivial to us when we find ourselves alone on a church-top, with the blue sky and a few tall pinnacles, and see far below us the steep roofs and foreshortened buttresses, and the silent activity of the city streets; but how much more must they not have seemed so to him as he stood, not only above other men's business, but above other men's climate, in a golden zone like Apollo's!

This was the sort of pleasure I found in the country of which I write. The pleasure was to be out of the wind, and to keep it in memory all the time, and hug oneself upon the shelter. And it was only by the sea that any such sheltered places were to be found. Between the black worm-eaten head-lands there are little bights and havens, well screened from the wind and the commotion of the external sea, where the sand and weeds look up into the gazer's face from a depth of tranquil water, and the sea-birds, screaming and flickering from the ruined crags, alone disturb the silence and the sunshine. One such place has impressed itself on my memory beyond all others. On a rock by the water's edge, old fighting men of the Norse breed had planted a double castle; the two stood wall to wall like semi-detached villas; and yet feud had run so high between their owners, that one, from out of a window, shot the other as he stood in his own doorway. There is something in the juxtaposition of these two enemies full of tragic irony. It is grim to think of bearded men and bitter women taking hateful counsel together about the two hall-fires at night, when the sea boomed against the foundations and the wild winter wind was loose over the battlements. And in the study we may reconstruct for ourselves some pale figure of what life then was. Not so when we are there; when we are there such thoughts come to us only to intensify a contrary impression, and association is turned against itself. I remember walking thither three afternoons in succession, my eyes weary with being set against the wind, and how, dropping suddenly over the edge of the down, I found myself in a new world of warmth and shelter. The wind, from which I had escaped, 'as from an enemy,' was seemingly quite local. It carried no clouds with it, and came from such a quarter that it did not trouble the sea within view. The two castles, black and ruinous as the rocks about them, were still distinguishable from these by something more insecure and fantastic in the outline, something that the last storm had left imminent and the next would demolish entirely. It would be difficult to render in words the sense of peace that took possession of me on these three afternoons. It was helped out, as I have said, by the contrast. The shore was battered and bemauled by previous tempests; I had the memory at heart of the insane strife of the pigmies who had erected these two castles and lived in them in mutual distrust and enmity, and knew I had only to put my head out of this little cup of shelter to find the hard wind blowing in my eyes; and yet there were the two great tracts of motionless blue air and peaceful sea looking on, unconcerned and apart, at the turmoil of the present moment and the memorials of the precarious past. There is ever something transitory and fretful in the impression of a high wind under a cloudless sky; it seems to have no root in the constitution of things; it must speedily begin to faint and wither away like a cut flower. And on those days the thought of the wind and the thought of human life came very near together in my mind. Our noisy years did indeed seem moments in the being of the eternal silence; and the wind, in the face of that great field of stationary blue, was as the wind of a butterfly's wing. The placidity of the sea was a thing likewise to be remembered. Shelley speaks of the sea as 'hungering for calm,' and in this place one learned to understand the phrase. Looking down into these green waters from the broken edge of the rock, or swimming leisurely in the sunshine, it seemed to me that they were enjoying their own tranquillity; and when now and again it was disturbed by a wind ripple on the surface, or the quick black passage of a fish far below, they settled back again (one could fancy) with relief.

On shore too, in the little nook of shelter, everything was so subdued and still that the least particular struck in me a pleasurable surprise. The desultory crackling of the whin-pods in the afternoon sun usurped the ear. The hot, sweet breath of the bank, that had been saturated all day long with sunshine, and now exhaled it into my face, was like the breath of a fellow-creature. I remember that I was haunted by two lines of French verse; in some dumb way they seemed to fit my surroundings and give expression to the contentment that was in me, and I kept repeating to myself—

> 'Mon coeur est un luth suspendu,
> Sitôt qu'on le touche, il résonne.'

I can give no reason why these lines came to me at this time; and for that very cause I repeat them here. For all I know, they may serve to complete the impression in the mind of the reader, as they were certainly a part of it for me.

And this happened to me in the place of all others where I liked least to stay. When I think of it I grow ashamed of my own ingratitude. 'Out of the strong came forth sweetness.' There, in the bleak and gusty North, I received, perhaps, my strongest impression of peace. I saw the sea to be great and calm; and the earth, in that little corner, was all alive and friendly to me. So, wherever a man is, he will find something to please and pacify him: in the town he will meet pleasant faces of men and women, and see beautiful flowers at a window, or hear a cage-bird singing at the corner of the gloomiest street; and for the country, there is no country without some amenity—let him only look for it in the right spirit, and he will surely find.

Lightning Source UK Ltd.
Milton Keynes UK
UKOW032358280512

193490UK00002B/110/P